SUCCESSFUL
SMALL
BUSINESS
MANAGEMENT

Leon A. Wortman

amacom A Division of
American Management Associations

Library of Congress Cataloging in Publication Data

Wortman, Leon A
  Successful small business management.

  1. Small business—Management.   I. Title.
HD69.S6W67   658' 022   76-18160
ISBN 0-8144-5394-5
ISBN 0-8144-7503-5 pbk

First AMACOM paperback edition 1978.
Fifteenth Printing

FOREWORD

ECONOMIC power is in the process of shifting to those who can cope with an accelerating rate of change in their environments. Coping with change means understanding and anticipating new technological development; and this, in turn, means acquiring, organizing, and utilizing knowledge itself or those people who possess knowledge. One of the primary requirements for entry into and survival in business is the acquisition of the technical and managerial skills needed to cope with rapid change.

Big business often owns the resources that attract those who already have, or who demonstrate the ability to acquire, managerial competence. The small-business owner, with necessarily narrow resources, usually finds that he cannot afford the high salaries, bonuses, perquisites, and superficial devices (such as plush offices) that may attract the experienced professional manager.

More often than not, the only course of action open to the owner or manager of the enterprise is to acquire the knowledge and develop the multiple skills within himself. He has to learn how to be a business manager. He has little time to teach, possibly little time for learning. However, if the business is to succeed, he must take or make time to assure his own technical education and managerial growth.

There are many definitions, many attempts to quantify the term "small business." The Small Business Act of 1953 defines "small business" in broad terms which say that such a firm is independently owned and operated and is not dominant in its field of operations. The Act also states that criteria used in defining a small business may vary from industry to industry.

A revised system for measuring the number of small businesses and their value throughout the economy has been under development by the Small Business Administration. Currently, SBA definitions of "small business" in the construction, services, wholesale, and retail industries are according to total or average annual receipts. For the manufacturing industries, the definitions are based on maximums for the average number of employees.

If the business owner or manager doesn't really know whether or not his is a "small" business, his technical and managerial problems are serious indeed. However, identification is made by the Small Business Administration whenever a company applies for specific aid under an SBA program, for example, financial, procurement, or investment assistance.

Data is available from the Internal Revenue Service which shows that the total number of all U.S. businesses, excluding farms, was approximately 9.7 million in 1972. The SBA converts this data, applying its own standards, to state that approximately 9.2 million of these can be defined as "small." Under proposed standards, this figure would be even higher. The census of business proprietorships shows there were 7.083 million proprietorships, 1.779 million corporations, and 0.880 million partnerships.

The title of this book makes it abundantly clear that its contents are directed to the 9.2 million small business owners and managers. They are growing in number every year, and their environments are growing in complexity. The small businessman has been with us no doubt from the very first time an early man exchanged or bartered goods, hopefully improving his lot, or from the very first time he received a reward for his original idea. We will never know who he was. Allow me to credit this unknown entrepreneur with having created the need for this book.

Allow me, too, to acknowledge the resources used in writing these pages. These resources include the people and publications of government agencies, especially of the Small Business Administration and the Department of Commerce. I am grateful, too, to the Main Library at Stanford University, to the Palo Alto Public Library and its dedicated librarians, and to the World Trade Library in San Francisco. Last, and exceptionally important, are the many managers and executives of "small" and "big" businesses who enabled me to learn from them by willingly sharing their practical knowledge or, in some cases, giving me the opportunity to learn the hard way—they hired me, some fired me, but every one of them was my teacher. And you know how teachers are.

Leon A. Wortman

CONTENTS

Introduction: What This Book Can Do for You   **1**

PART ONE
PLANNING AND CONTROLLING

   1 Why Is a Business Plan Essential?   **7**
   2 How To Develop a Plan   **11**
   3 How To Record Your Progress   **25**
   4 Organize Your Growth   **35**
   5 Successful Recruiting and Training   **41**

PART TWO
ACCOUNTING, FINANCE, AND MANAGEMENT

   6 Money Has Its Own Language   **55**
   7 Break Through the Profit Barrier   **61**
   8 Reduce Costs and Increase Profits   **71**
   9 Depreciate Your Assets   **81**
  10 Danger Signals in Cost Estimating   **89**
  11 Are You Pricing for Profit?   **95**
  12 Pricing, Competition, and the Law   **111**

13 How to Read Financial Statements **123**
14 What's Your Return on Investment? **137**
15 How to Use Ratios to Measure Your Success **143**
16 How Much Cash Do You Need? **157**
17 How to Determine the Kind of Money You Need **167**
18 Do You Know Your Sources of Financing? **173**

PART THREE
MARKETING AND SALES

19 Forecasting Sales: Key to the Front Door **183**
20 How to Select, Train, and Motivate Good
      Salesmen **197**
21 How the Professional Salesman Manages
      Time and Territory **211**
22 How to Understand Sale and Payment Terms **217**
23 How to Expand Sales through Account Analysis **223**
24 How to Create a Positive Image **229**
25 Growth Opportunities through Export Sales **239**
26 How to Be Your Own Management Consultant **247**

Afterword **251**

Index **253**

Introduction:
What This Book
Can Do for You

THE very fact that you are reading this page indicates you are or expect to be the owner or manager of a business. Some of you will make it go. Some will fail. According to statistics, upwards of 82 percent of all new business ventures fail within the first two years of their operation. You are reading this because you intend to be among the 18 percent who survive, and you will work diligently to be among the still smaller percentage of those who show a profit.

Here are figures quoted by the Small Business Administration on the underlying causes of business failures; the data varies little from year to year:

Lack of experience in their line	9%
Lack of management experience	18
Unbalanced experience	20
Incompetence	45
Neglect	3
Fraud	2
Disaster	1
Unknown	2
Total	100%

The statistics are so dramatically definitive that it becomes relatively simple to know which danger signals to observe and where to put the learning emphasis. We can assume you will dedicate your energies to the business and are honest beyond doubt; so, we eliminate neglect and fraud immediately as significant danger zones and we concentrate on building your skills as a competent, well-balanced manager.

It isn't easy. There is no formula for management that guarantees success. However, there are some basics, some time-tested fundamentals that can significantly improve the probabilities for survival and for generating profits. This book is written specifically for those present and future business managers who are willing to do some reading and acquire practical knowledge of the less romantic aspects of running a business. By "less romantic" we refer to pragmatic, noncreative needs, such as keeping meaningful records, doing financial reporting and analysis, and controlling the tangibles.

It doesn't matter what kind of business you are in or are starting. The nontechnical everyday language of this book applies to manufacturing, wholesaling, distributing, retailing, marketing, and selling a service or a product. In every business you add value—to time in the form of a service rendered, or to materials in the form of labor to produce a component or a product. In the process of adding value you have every right to expect to receive a profitable return on your investment in time, labor, and materials.

It is astonishing to discover that many business managers do not know whether or not their operations are profitable. Worse, they do not know how to determine the results of their efforts—until it may be too late. This book helps you plan and control for profitable end results. It helps you establish the methods and bench marks for determining profit or loss. It talks facts that you will recognize as valid. In fact, you may already be using some of them in your business. If so, this book will help you derive more benefits from the good practices. Possibly you discarded some of the practices as being meaningless It is expected that reading about them in these pages will provide you with a new, more positive perspective about their applications and values.

No doubt you are reading this book because you want to make things and your own future better than they are. If your venture is in the start-up phase, you want to get off on the right foot. Bravo!

In the pages that follow are the techniques and practices, *not theories,* that have helped many managers make decisions and take actions to steer their businesses in profitable directions. They are the techniques and practices of successful small-business management.

PART ONE

*planning
and
controlling*

1

Why Is a Business Plan Essential?

"WHY did this happen to me?" This is too often the reaction of the small businessman forced to close his shop. He means it. The surprise, the mystery is genuine. He really doesn't know what happened to him. Unfortunately, his track record as a business manager is severely damaged. If he were to develop resources adequate to a new start-up, what do you suppose might be his chances for success? Ask his creditors, the local lending agency, or his banker. It's not very likely they will be enthusiastic about extending credit or making a loan for a new start-up. Then, again, if Mr. Failure has learned a lesson and if he can articulate the facts and display a document called *a new business plan,* Mr. Lender and Mr. Creditor may back him.

It happens all the time. We read about Mr. Smith opening a business. It closes. Mr. Smith manages to reopen, perhaps in another location or even in another business. Mr. Smith appears to be virtually indestructible, certainly energetic, but continually failing. Why not successful? His probabilities for success would improve immeasurably if he would stop racing about just long enough to analyze the facts that the overwhelming majority of failures are the result of poorly prepared, poorly informed, or poorly organized management. Mr. Smith wants success so badly he can taste it. But he never even gets close enough to touch it. Mr. Smith, in his immaturity, confuses "objective" with "plan." He behaves like the enthusiastic youth who at age 18 vows to be a millionaire by the time he is 30. At 30 he moves the objective out to age 40. Then to 50 and so on.

What is missing? Why is he never fulfilled? Actually there is nothing wrong with the objective, despite statistical improbabilities of achievement. The major, missing element is a *plan* that would detail the method by which he would achieve the *objective* of becoming a millionaire. Mr. Smith has enthusiasm but no programs, no score cards. And you can't tell the winners from the losers without one or the other.

Large businesses have in-depth management. Lots of titles fulfill many functions essential to the achievement of corporate goals. Small businesses have in-depth management, too. The major difference is that in the small operation one or two people may carry all the titles, wear all the management hats. If some of the titles and functions in the large business do not match each other well enough, changes can be made without destroying the organization. However, in the small business, heads cannot be changed so readily. The small-business manager must have a dynamic head size, one that can instantly retract or expand to fit and fill the hat. Large businesses have almost unlimited internal resources and specialized talent available for every conceivable situation or emergency. Obviously, the small-business manager has to be considerably more versatile than any of the managers of a large business.

The chief executive of a large business faced with an important decision calls a meeting of his top management. These specialists convene and, in due time, define the problem, state and analyze the alternative solutions, decide on the course of action that offers the greatest probability for success, and initiate the action. On the other hand, the small-business manager is literally on his own. Yet he must go through the same essential processes of problem definition, analysis, resolution, and course of action.

The operation of an independent enterprise, a small business, is probably one of the toughest challenges an individual can accept. The entrepreneur who thinks he will be really independent when he becomes his own boss might be sorely disappointed. The fact is, the small-business manager has quite a few bosses, many more than he may realize. These include:

Local, state, and federal regulatory agencies.
The suppliers who control his materials flow.
Financial backers and creditors.
Customers.
Market conditions, cycles, and seasons.
Personal and family demands.

No, independent business is not the place for the immature, the weak, or those who intend to take it easy. It is the place for those who can plan, organize, direct, coordinate, and control, as well as work hard, long hours.

"Why did this happen to me?"

Probably there was no firm, definitive *plan*. And without a plan, what was there to organize, direct, coordinate, or control? Without a plan, how is one to know where he is supposed to be going, how to get there, what to do about delays, obstacles, and hazards? The small-business manager can be the most committed person on earth but without the technical commitment, the physical business plan, he and his business become a boat with a powerful, throbbing engine, but without charts, without a steering mechanism.

One should not think of launching a new business, large or small, without a business plan. The plan is the tool for plotting a course for the company, a logical progression from starting point to ending point.

The neophyte, the untested, and those who have experienced business failure may be thinking: "Why should I draw

up a business plan? It takes time. What's in it for me?"
A business plan provides many benefits. Four of the most
important are the following:

□ A plan describes a path for you to follow. A plan with
goals, targets, bench marks, timetables, strategies, tactics,
programs, policies can guide your business optimally
through periods of growth, safeguard its survival during risk
periods and recessions, improve your recognition of opportunities, and act as a true compass when visibility is poor.

□ A plan enables your bankers and creditors to understand and appreciate your potential for successful small-
business management. Reading or listening to the details of
your plan provides them with useful, ready insight into your
situation when their aid is needed.

□ A plan serves as a definitive communications tool
when you need to orient personnel and suppliers about your
operations, specific goals, and realistic ambitions.

□ A plan can help you develop your own managerial
skills. It serves superbly as an organized approach to defining your personal assets and liabilities; describing competitive and marketing conditions, financial and facilities needs,
staff and payroll requirements; and predicting problems and
solutions. The well-developed plan helps you know what
can happen, prepares you so that you can minimize risk and
maximize opportunity.

2

How to Develop
a Plan

DO you recall the old one that goes, "We are a non-profit organization. We didn't plan it that way, but that's the way it worked out"? An assumption is made that you are already in business or are going into business to make a profit: to make money by manufacturing and selling a product, or by buying and reselling a product made by someone else, or by providing a useful service. You are dedicated to making a profit and to making it work out that way. Fine. A plan is essential, so let's go about the task of developing your own business plan.

Now is the time for complete honesty with yourself. In developing a *plan* you must face facts about who and what you really are, your skills, assets, and deficiencies. It's soul-searching time. What's your real motivation for going into business for yourself? What makes you think you are competent as a small-business manager? Can you recognize your own shortcomings or have you been blaming the world for your failures? It may be hard to take.

Self-criticism is what it's all about. An honest evaluation of your personality and your skills. Why? Simply so that you can determine whether or not you are emotionally and philosophically fitted to small business or to management. Also, and at least as important, you must openly face a recognition of your own limitations. Each of us has limitations. Nothing to be ashamed about, unless you won't admit them to yourself. By defining, describing, and spelling out your limitations as well as your assets, by preparing a personal balance sheet in which you describe your pluses and credits in one column, your minuses and debits in another column, you can determine whether or not you are equipped to go it alone. Ignoring the financial picture for the moment, such a personal balance sheet can be of enormous help in determining whether or not you need a partner, or partners, to round out the "skills and competence" department of your business venture.

It must be noted that this "balance sheet" approach to the business plan is not restricted in value to those not yet actively in business. It is just as important to the success of a business that is already in operation.

You may be very strong in marketing and sales skills, weak in engineering, manufacturing, or finance, for example. It could be prudent and significantly improve your probabilities for success to join hands with another individual whose talents, skills, and strengths complement your own. Be very much aware of the point made earlier that the small-business manager must be equipped to wear many hats, fulfill many functions that are normally dispersed among many individuals and titles in the large corporation.

Now that you have completed the personal balance sheet, you must move on to a number of other evaluations of business conditions. Here, too, honesty with yourself is exceptionally important. It is imperative that you divorce emotion from facts as you continue to develop your business plan. You may really be turned on by the kind of business you contemplate or are already into. But, because the name of the game is profit measured in genuine dollars, you must become as objective as possible. Stick to facts. Know what advantages you have to start with. Know what others it takes to succeed.

Starting and running a small business is risky, but your chances of making it go will be improved if you understand the problems you may meet and if you work out solutions for as many of them as you can from the very beginning. The plan begins with questions only you can answer, or answers which only you must find.

What business am I in? It may sound silly to ask yourself this one because you may have already spent many productive years in it and you take your knowledge for granted. There's the rub! Taking anything for granted can be dangerous at this point. You must be able to spell out, for yourself and for other important people, just what your business is or will be. Suppose your intention is to buy and resell electronic semiconductor devices. Is that your business? Or are you really intending to become a distributor or dealer in electronic components, offering a broad range of items from resistors through electronic hardware, capacitors, transformers, wire, and all the other items related to the sale and use of semiconductors? If your real intent is to concentrate on semiconductors, that's fine. Just as long as you recognize that you are proposing to become a specialist, not a general supplier of families of components. Spell it out precisely.

What are the marketing conditions and requirements? When you specified the nature of your business, you made the first marketing decision: What? Now you are ready to move to details of why? when? where? and how? Define your products, your customers, and your competition.

If a production capability is part of your program, you have to decide who your market is, where it is, why customers will buy your product instead of your competitors'. Is the market growing, shrinking, static? Why is it that way? Are there any seasonal aspects to the buying habits? Is the market cyclical? How big is the total market and what percentage of it are you aiming for in the first, second, and third years? With this information in hand you can begin to document the size of your facility and storage space and the types and quantities of production machinery, and, of course, you can begin to describe the numbers of production people and the skills that will be required for operations.

What classification do I fit? You will want to do some basic research to obtain facts and figures about the products and about the customers you want to reach.

A good source of such facts is the Standard Industrial Classification (SIC) directories of products and industries. The SIC classifies firms by the type of activity in which they are engaged. It is used by virtually all government agencies—federal, state and local—to develop uniformity that enables comparisons of statistical data. The *Standard Industrial Classification Manual* is available from the Superintendent of Documents, U.S. Government Printing Office, Washington, D.C. 20402. Many local public libraries have copies at the reference desk.

Quantitative information accumulated and published by city, county, state, and federal agencies usually refers to an industry according to the SIC. Once you have found the SIC code for your business, you will be able to use the large number of publications available at most libraries in determining important market facts about your competition and the size of your industry.

What is my market area? Geographically, physically, to whom are you going to offer your products and services? Do you intend to concentrate on a neighborhood, city, county, state, region, the entire country, or international market? Describe your territories of business on paper and use maps as an aid. There are many maps and charts available with statistical information, such as numbers of households, retail sales, industrial capital budgets, populations, and businesses for any territory you propose to reach. Several sources of marketing data are described in the last part of this book. Obtain and use the facts as a guide to planning on the basis of solid numerical information rather than conjecture such as "There must be lots of people out there who can use what I make."

Who are my competitors? After defining your territory of activity, list as many competitors or potential competitors as are known to you and as you can find in the *SIC Manual*. If hard data is not available, estimate as best you can the dollar sales achieved by each of your competitors in the marketplace. Total them and, because you did some earlier homework, figure the dollars and percentage of market you intend to achieve. Estimate whether your achievement in dollars and your growth in the next three years will be the result of taking business away from your competition or of market growth. Perhaps it will be a combination of their loss and an increase in market size. Know where your business, your sales dollars, will come from.

What are the strengths and weaknesses of my competitors? In answering this question, use a combination of whatever reliable data is available to you, opinions of customers and associates in whom you have confidence, and, of course, your own opinion based on your personal experience in the industry or with products and services of a like nature. Review the ways in which your competitors advertise, promote sales, distribute their products, market their capabilities.

Consider their response time to orders. Is it slow, fast, adequate? Why is it the way it is? What is your competition's ability to respond to changing market conditions? What is the need for new products or new services? Have any of your competitors folded in the past year, and, if so, what were the reasons? Are they trying to reopen? Why? How? When?

What advantages do I have over my competitors? Because you evaluated your competition's strengths and weaknesses it should be easy to list the basis on which you will capture a share of the market. Make a checklist of your competitors' products or services that permits a rapid comparison of the areas in which you have an advantage. Analyze each feature or characteristic carefully. Try to be objective.

In determining your advantages, recognize that a lower price for your offering may not be an advantage for you if your quality is lower. Think in terms of price/value relationships.

What does the customer get for his money? The more detailed you make your checklist, the more useful it will be in evaluating your status.

Use the same checklist, or make a second one, to indicate the areas in which you have a notable disadvantage. Then use a separate sheet to describe the disadvantage *and* what you intend to do about converting it to an advantage. Put a star alongside those features of your products or services which are unique. Describe why they are unique. What is the probability or possibility of a competitor catching up? How long will it take him to catch up? Are you protected by a patent or copyright? If not, can you be?

How do I propose to distribute my product or deliver my services? This really means, How will I get my offerings to the customers? You must describe the several ways in which you can accomplish this goal. Sell direct? Store pickup? Personal delivery? Mail or freight services? Would you use floor or desk salesmen? Field salesmen? Would you compensate them by salary or commission? Would you sell through manufacturers' reps? Distributors? Dealers? Brokers? What about support through advertising, sales promotion, and merchandising programs?

At this point you must do more than just list and describe the various ways available for completing the marketing cycle. You must consider comparative costs of magazine, newspaper, radio, TV, direct mail advertising, circulars, broadsides, flyers, mailers, handouts, posters, price sheets, and other types of literature essential to getting your message across. The kind, quantity, and quality of these marketing-support tools will vary in accordance with the method of distribution and the size of your proposed territory. Describe any special marketing or merchandising programs or techniques normally used in your industry. These facts will be needed when you develop the financial segments of your business plan.

What are the essential manufacturing operations? List and describe the basic steps in manufacturing your products or in completing your services. For example, cutting, sewing, machining, shaping, soldering, painting, assembling, testing, packaging, and so on. This information, too, will be vital in assessing your financial needs for production equipment.

What are my sources of supply? Know where your suppliers are. It is as important as knowing where your customers are. Make certain you know the locations of primary and secondary sources of supplies of raw materials, components, subassemblies, and other materials and services. How dependable are they? What kind of delivery schedule are they on? This will help you determine lead time for ordering materials. What are their standard terms and conditions? This will help you determine your cash needs for purchased goods and services.

Do I know my labor needs? For each piece of machinery or equipment you will have in your operations, you will need specific skills and numbers of people, including your own shop time. List and describe the skills, the levels of competence of the people you will have to employ. And, where will you get them? Is there a pool of skilled labor, ready to produce, or will you have to train unskilled labor to do your job?

What is the turnover rate typical of the kind of people you will employ? This has a distinct effect on labor cost. Each time you replace an employee, you incur the costs associated with the learning curve to achieve full productivity. Investigate regulations related to the environment in which your people will work. Your equipment, facilities, and method of operation must comply with the Occupational Safety and Health Act of 1970. Not all labor is part of the production capability. Don't forget to include bookkeepers even though they may work part-time, accountants even if they are not on the payroll, receptionists, typists, and the switchboard if you are big enough to require one.

Do I know my space needs? There is something puzzling or pathetic about seeing a building whose interior is significantly less than 100 percent utilized. The old saw about room for expansion is very unconvincing. It is wasteful, a sign of poor planning or of retrenchment, to have oversized facilities. Planning for immediate, midterm, and long-term space requirements is not only financially prudent but an immediate indicator of good management.

Follow the example of the vendor who kept his overhead down by operating out of a pushcart, then rented a small store into which he put more merchandise carefully selected for fast turnover on the basis of his experience in buying and selling from the pushcart. As profits were generated, he leased the storefront space next door, expanded into the next and the next, took over the whole street frontage, and finally bought the buildings to launch a flourishing department store.

Yes, know your space needs. Describe them on paper in relation to your earlier estimates of growth in the next one, two, and three years. Select a site that, among other things, enables you to expand the space to fit the need. In planning your space, include realistic square-footage estimates of office, production, storage, and shipping facilities. Rest room and parking space requirements, of course, must be taken into account. Talk to the local building inspectors about local ordinances so that you can avoid any surprises that might result in unplanned expenses.

How about a partner? If you have determined the need for one or more partners with money or know-how to complement your own resources, do you know people who will fit your special situation? Have you discussed it with them? Have you eliminated or included them in your plans? Have you talked to a lawyer about the form your business will take? Think out carefully and realistically what aspects of the work would be within the skills of your potential partners. Discuss it with them and make certain you and they understand the full meaning of the commitment to success.

What image do I want to create? Like it or not, your business, servicing or manufacturing or selling, will develop an image. The way people will think of your company and the repeatability of their business with you will be influenced by the way you conduct your affairs.

You can control that image. If people come to your place for service, for example, such things as the cleanliness of the environment, friendliness, and the manner in which they are treated can be just as important to whether or not they come back again as is the quality of your work or product. Pleasant, prompt, courteous service before and after the sale will help make satisfied customers your best form of advertising—your image builder. Your business plan must include a description of what image you intend to develop *and* how you propose to create and maintain it. This is the time to lay down your basic policies and principles on how to handle customers and their problems, and how to provide proper solutions. Remember, it costs more money to make the first sale than it does to make the second or follow-on sales to a customer. It costs considerably more to find a new customer than it does to maintain an old one.

Cash or credit? One of your goals is to put cash into the strongbox. If you have operated with your customers on a cash basis, consider the impact on business if you extend credit. Americans like to buy on credit or, in retail purchases, with a charge card. Consider whether or not a system of credit and collections will add to your business growth, attract and hold customers. Often the customer will make the "buy" decision more rapidly or purchase now something he intended to acquire later, when he is enabled to use credit at your place of business.

Plan your money requirements. The financial part of your plan obviously demands serious, careful, thorough attention to detail. Use a columnar accounting pad or any sheet on which you can draw vertical columns and horizontal lines. Accounting requirements will vary from business to business and according to the size or complexity of the business. If you do not have a financial, accounting, or bookkeeping background, it would be wise to consult with a certified public accountant, preferably one who is not related to you so that he can offer total objectivity. A competent accountant brought in at the start is well worth his fee. He can save you time, headaches, and expenses for which you may otherwise be totally unprepared. A C.P.A. will help you set up the accounting system best suited to your specific needs. However, you must make the overall financial plan yourself and prepare some basic but specific dollar and timetable data with which he will work. You will find it easiest for you and your accountant to communicate when you prepare a sheet of data as in Figure 1.

Wherever possible, do research to provide facts and hard dollar information. Where research is not practicable, make your best estimate. Err on the high side for expenses, the low

Figure 1. Data sheet for estimating monthly expenses.

Item	Month #1 (1)	Month #2 (2)	Mont	#10	Month #11 (11)	Month #12 (12)	First 12 months totals (13)
Salary – partner 1							
Salary – partner 2							
All other salaries							
Commissions*							
Bonuses*							
Rent							
Telephone							
Utilities							
Delivery Truck							
Postage							
Advertising							
Printing costs							
Interest on loans							
Equipment rentals							
Production materials							
Tools							
Fixtures							
Office supplies							
Legal fees (retainers)							
Accountant (retainers)							
Travel expenses							
Business entertainment							
Organization costs							
Remodeling							
Deposits (utilities)							
Deposits (rentals)							
Licenses and permits							
Miscellaneous							
Totals							

DW Company

Estimated Expenses from Start _____ 19__

	INITIALS	DATE
PREPARED BY		
APPROVED BY		

*To be paid out of income

side for income. Short-circuit the tendency to do the opposite in an effort to convince yourself that you can start on the
proverbial shoestring. Perhaps you can, but it is best to know
from the start whether or not you might be able to stretch the
shoestring far enough.

Just as you did with expenses and start-up cash, you must
program or estimate your orders and sales (shipments) plan.
This is essential to determining when and if you will begin to
make a profit. Figure 2 illustrates a method that displays the
anticipated orders and sales flow in dollars. It refers to
known, specific accounts. It includes your best forecast of
business that can be realistically expected to develop within
the charted period. The "period" should display the next 12
months, month-to-month. On separate sheets for both expenses and income, it is important to display forecasts for the
second 12-month period, on a quarterly basis. Carry it a step
further and forecast your position for the third year without
attempting to break it down to intervals.

**Figure 2. Data sheet with anticipated monthly orders and
sales.**

DW Company							INITIALS	DATE
						PREPARED BY		
Orders/Sales Forecast from _____ 19__						APPROVED BY		
	(1)	(2)		#10	(11)	(12)	(15)	
	Month #1 $	Month #2 $	Mont		Month #11 $	Month #12 $	First 12 months $ totals	
Orders								
Company A	249.00	1,258.00	1,11	00	3,680.00	4,000.00	14,206.00	
B	− 00	326.00	50	00	1,250.00	1,500.00	7,258.00	
C	127.00	943.00	1,20	00	2,750.00	2,750.00	12,850.00	
D	− 00	− 00	9	00	1,500.00	1,750.00	11,750.00	
Misc. accounts	100.00	225.00	9	00	500.00	750.00	2,500.00	
Totals	476.00	2,752.00	4,19	00	9,680.00	10,750.00	48,564.00	
Sales (shipments)								
Company A	− 00	175.00	1,11	00	3,200.00	3,680.00	13,975.00	
B	− 00	− 00	1	00	1,100.00	1,250.00	7,000.00	
C	− 00	127.00	10	00	2,000.00	2,750.00	12,000.00	
D	− 00	− 00		00	1,250.00	1,500.00	11,000.00	
Misc. accounts	− 00	100.00	1	00	400.00	500.00	2,250.00	
Totals	− 00	402.00	2,70	00	7,950.00	9,680.00	46,225.00	

Of course, as your anticipated orders and shipment rates grow, you must replan your requirements for facilities, equipment, personnel, and all the overhead items that will be affected. You may discover some mind-boggling phenomena such as your debts growing as rapidly as your sales, or even more rapidly. When you observe this numerical situation, review the profitability of your operation as you expect it to grow. Will it generate enough cash and profit to meet your debts, loans, and other financial commitments? Can you expect your creditors to give attractive terms that will enable you to make your collections on sales in time to meet your obligations? Do you expect to be doing business with customers who pay promptly or will you have a perpetual cash shortage caused by collection problems?

Perhaps you will want to chart your financial position out to five years. Perhaps you will find it essential or valuable to detail the second year of operations on a month-to-month basis. How you do it, the amount of detail you develop, will become obvious to you as you plot the first 12 months.

If it still appears that cash problems will develop during the period of your specific plan, don't be disheartened. Go back over the numbers several times, searching for ways in which to reduce expenses without significantly reducing orders and sales. This is a superb exercise in cost reduction, an exercise you will be engaging in many times, all during your business management career. Further into this book there are chapters on finance and borrowing that will be helpful when it is indicated that an infusion of cash, in the form of a loan, is essential to growth and profitability. Plotting your break-even point is important, too, as a bench mark in your determined march to profit. A chapter is dedicated to a method for computing your break-even dollars in a simplified and effective way.

Thus, when all the soul-searching is done, when you have completely dissected your objectives and personal goals, when you have done the fundamental arithmetic of your fiscal future, you will have developed a plan for successful business management. As much as is practicable, you will have forecasted your problems, developed some solutions. You will be ready to do one of several things: delay action while you refine your plan, quit (not likely at this stage), or proceed with a feeling of confidence that, short of pretending to be a psychic, you know as much about your future as any mortal possibly can.

3

How to Record
Your Progress

KEEPING records is as important to the small-business manager as it is to the big-business executive. Records of every aspect of the business operation are essential to keeping score of the day-to-day progress of your business plan. It is surprising but true that many business managers do not know the current score of their own businesses, either because of inadequate records or because the records are not kept up to date.

The cliché is, "You can't tell the players without a scorecard." A business manager or executive without his scorecards can't tell whether he's winning, losing, or breaking even. He can't even tell whether or not he has a problem. He is unable to make sensible decisions. Another cliché compares a manager without adequate records with a gunslinger whose gun has no sights—thus, the business manager who "shoots from the hip." If he sprays enough bullets in rapid-fire sequence, he might hit the target. But, while he is hip-shooting, the return fire can be devastating! It is no mere coincidence that more often than not a bank-rupted small business is guilty, among other things, of not maintaining adequate records.

Adequate records are necessary to prepare tax returns. But, in reality, that is only a very small part of the value that an effective record keeping system offers. Accurate, complete, and current records are required by banks and other financial institutions with which you may deal. Your key suppliers and creditors may insist on financial reports of your business before they will support you. No matter how well you may appear to be doing, there is nothing so positive and so convincing as a well-prepared, well-maintained set of books. Consider them essential, not just desirable. Records help you carry on your management activities in buying, selling, problem solving, and planning for the future. Records are a vital part of your management information system.

A record keeping system, to be useful, must be simple to use, easy to understand, reliable, accurate, and timely. Hard-number records will help keep you out of trouble and provide you with facts for making sound decisions. The kind and complexity of the record keeping system you institute depends on the nature of your operation. For example, the part-time vendor who sells bags of peanuts at the ball game has a very simple inventory control record. He estimates the number of bags of peanuts he needs for one game. A quick glance at his tray when the ball park closes tells him the story of his day's movement of merchandise. One item of inventory, one day of business. His maintenance and operating expenses are likewise easily determined, being mostly the cost of cleaning his uniform and cap.

We assume, however, that your business is somewhat more complex. Even if it means you are managing a group of peanut vendors covering several games each day or week, your records have to be considerably more comprehensive, matching the size of your total investment and the fact that your business is on-going throughout the year.

In this chapter, descriptions are given for different kinds of records, according to their use. Some may not apply to your specific venture, while others are basic and absolutely essential. These may call your attention to some types of records you might have overlooked but could use to great advantage. Consult with your accountant about the kinds of records you should keep. This is important. He will need your "books" to prepare critical documents such as balance sheets, profit-and-loss statements, and tax returns.

Every firm needs an accounting system to safeguard assets and minimize errors in decision making. It must be honestly and accurately maintained by those responsible for keeping the books. The system should be so designed that no employee has complete control of any business transaction. For example, employees handling cash should not keep the account books. Those working as cashiers or active in collecting cash accounts should not also keep the records of these accounts. The person authorizing purchases should be someone other than the bookkeeper.

The bookkeeping process is based on several major groups of information:

Original documents record transactions when they are made, including sales slips, receiving records, invoices, checks, and time cards.

Journals are formal books that display transactions in chronological order together with the credits and debits involved. A general journal records all transactions. There may also be one or more special journals for specific classes of transactions such as sales, purchasing, and cash.

The ledger records the increases or decreases in various assets, liabilities, capital, distribution of ownerships, income and expenses. Any book or file in which a number of accounts are accumulated is known as a ledger.

Trial balances double-check all entries in the ledger to make certain all are in good order and do balance. The trial balance is taken as close to the end of a business period as is possible, shortly after the end of the month, for example.

Financial statements are prepared once the trial balance is taken. Statements of profit and loss should be completed no later than ten days after the close of the business period so that they can be read, discussed with the accountant, digested, and converted to any necessary actions before the next business period is very far along.

Inventory and Purchasing Records

Inventory control records are essential to making the buy and sell decisions. Some companies control their stock by taking physical inventories at frequent intervals, monthly or quarterly. Others use a dollar inventory record that gives a rough idea of what the inventory may be from day to day in terms of dollars. If your stock is primarily made up of thousands of different items, as it would be in a variety store, you may find *dollar control* more practicable than *physical control*. However, even in this example, a physical inventory count must be taken periodically to verify the levels of inventory by item.

Perpetual item inventory control records are practicable for those selling big-ticket items. In such examples it is quite suitable to hand-count the starting inventory, maintain a card for each item or for each group of items, and reduce the item count each time a unit is sold or transferred out of inventory. Still, periodic physical counts are taken to verify the accuracy of the inventory cards.

Out-of-stock sheet, sometimes called a "want sheet," notifies the buyer that it is time to reorder an item. Experience with the rate of turnover of an item will probably indicate the low level of inventory at which the unit should be reordered to assure receipt of new merchandise before the stock is totally exhausted.

Open-to-buy record helps you prevent ordering more than is needed to meet buyers' demands. This record adjusts your order rate to your sales rate. It provides a running account of the dollar amount that may be bought without departing significantly from the pre-established inventory levels.

Purchase order file keeps track of what has been ordered

and the status or expected receipt date for the materials. It is convenient to maintain this file by using a carbon copy of each purchase order you write. Notations can be added or information updated directly on the copy of the purchase order with respect to changes in prices or delivery dates.

Supplier file is a valuable reference on your suppliers, helpful in negotiating price, delivery, and terms. Extra copies of your purchase orders can be used to establish this record, alphabetically by supplier, which then serves to enable you to determine rapidly the amount of business you do with any of your suppliers.

Returned goods file provides a continuous record of merchandise you have returned to suppliers. It indicates amounts, dates, and reasons. This information is useful in controlling debits, credits, and quality.

Price book, maintained in alphabetical order according to your suppliers, provides a record of purchase prices, selling prices, markdowns and markups. It is important to keep this record completely up to date so that you are able rapidly to access the latest price and profit information on materials purchased for resale.

Sales Records

Individual sales transactions should be recorded to enable you to account for the outward flow of goods. If you use a cash register for sales transactions, you should have a sales slip and a cash register tape for all merchandise leaving your premises. Sales slips should be prenumbered and each number accounted for or marked "void" and initialed.

Summary of daily sales, based on the individual sales transaction record, can be accumulated into weekly or monthly charts or tables to disclose trends or cyclical buying habits. You can use the same information, when it is coded according to individual sales persons, to calibrate the effectiveness of your sales staff.

Operating plan, similar to the technique used in developing your overall business plan, sets up goals for sales during a specific short-term period—a week, month, season or a special sales promotion event—and permits a comparison with actuals. The same type of plan can be established for any aspect of your business—inventory control or controllable expenses, for example. The data for *plan* and *actual* are compared in a record called the "operating summary." Operating plans should be established for individual departments and for the entire business.

Accountability records display the pure fact of whether or not your business is making money or meeting plan. Also, they can help in management decision making by displaying profit-and-loss information by department or item, depending on how sophisticated or complex you want to be. By subtracting the purchase cost of items from the price at which they were sold, you derive *gross profit*. From this gross profit data, subtract expenses to arrive at *net profit* before taxes.

Some firms go so far as to keep a profit-and-loss record for each salesperson to determine the productivity in profit-dollars for the individual. Bear in mind, however, that this is only one technique for measuring sales performance. It is not always feasible or realistic to evaluate a salesperson in terms of net profit without giving him control over those things that affect profit. It is practicable to establish accountability records for each department and for each major item or service that is sold.

Cash Records

Daily cash reconciliation provides data in summary form for entry into your cash-receipts journal. All cash-received data, such as can be accessed from cash-register tapes or payments in any form that may have been delivered to your operation, is reconciled according to the beginning-of-the-day and the end-of-the-day balances.

Cash-receipts journal lists all the cash coming into your

business and its source. The amounts entered in this journal should be deposited intact in the bank. Never use cash receipts for paying bills. Pay them by check so that you have an official record of payment or, if the amount is relatively small, from your petty cash fund.

Petty cash fund can be used to cover such items as postage, freight, stationery supplies, and other miscellaneous expenses. Establish a ceiling on individual transactions that may be paid out of petty cash. It is typical to set the maximum single withdrawal from petty cash at $25. Each withdrawal should be covered by a voucher which states date, amount, purpose of withdrawal, and the signature or initials of the person making the withdrawal. Controls should be placed on the petty cash box, limiting access to one reliable employee in case you are unavailable when petty cash is needed for some purchase. At all times the cash in the petty cash box plus the receipts for withdrawals must equal the amount of the fund.

Bank reconciliation is performed to determine whether your firm's checkbook stubs agree with the bank's records of canceled checks. The bank's monthly statement should be compared with your records to assure that deposits as well as withdrawals agree with your checkbook, bankbook, and the general ledger.

Credit records, including charge account applications and credit limits by customer, help control your risk and exposure to losses due to nonpayment of accounts receivable. The data may be listed in simplified form according to name, or account number to provide anonymity, and is supported by individual files which reveal all facts known about the account's past performance in meeting obligations to pay bills.

Accounts receivable aging list shows the amount due and length of time a customer takes to make payments beyond your normal terms. It alerts you to potential cash flow problems in operating your business and indicates which accounts are potentially bad debts. This record is kept on a monthly basis, dating from the month an account was due and payable and showing how old it is at the current month. Bottom-line summaries of these accounts indicate to you the average age of your accounts or how long it takes to complete a collection.

Employee Records

Records of employee earnings and withholdings are essential in preparing tax returns and providing employees with Form W-2 withholding tax statements and corresponding state tax forms. The record should also keep track of amounts withheld for Social Security.

Employee's withholding exemption certificates should be recorded in support of the withholding exemptions claimed by your employees and as the basis for the deductions you make on their behalf. The law requires employees to file new exemption certificates, if there has been a change in their exemption status.

Hours worked record for each nonexempt employee proves your compliance with the law on minimum wages and overtime. This record is also useful in keeping track of payroll expenses, absences, latenesses, and vacation time.

Expense allowances and reimbursements to yourself and your employees for expenses incurred in connection with the job should be recorded. This is valuable in controlling out-of-pocket expenses and in supporting income tax deductions. Maintain a file of corresponding receipts for individual expense items over $25.

Employment applications maintained on file for each applicant hired can be used to prove good faith if employment is challenged by authorities.

Job descriptions should be written for each job in your operations. (Try writing one for yourself.) Give a copy to each new job candidate and new employee to assure that you have fully explained what is expected of the employee, the scope of his responsibility and authority, and to whom he reports.

Reasons for terminations should be noted and filed in the event of a challenge or in contesting claims for unemployment compensation.

Record of employee benefits is valuable in providing you with hard facts on what the true costs of personnel are. Costs should be spelled out for each employee's group medical plan, insurance, retirement, pension, paid holidays, paid vacations, and paid sick leave.

Performance appraisal records enable you to track an employee's work performance and habits on the job. Such a record, reviewed periodically with the individual employee, is helpful in discussing progress or the lack of progress and the granting or refusal of pay increases.

Fixtures and Property

Equipment records are essential in preparing income tax returns and in determining insurance coverage. This record shows the nature of each piece of capital equipment, the date acquired, how acquired, acquisition cost, estimated life, and method of depreciation.

Insurance records are related to equipment records and provide an accurate and convenient means for reviewing insurance coverage. When insurance policies are issued, this record shows policy numbers, insurers' names, type and amount of coverage, expiration and premium-due dates, and the dollar amount of the premium.

Control Your Accounts Receivable

It is vital to your lifeblood, the money flow, to observe a few rules that will help keep your accounts receivable current. Be sure that bills are prepared when goods are shipped or service is rendered. Avoid delay by making sure that correct mail addresses are used on documents and envelopes.

Monitor your *accounts receivable aging list* closely and determine the reason why each account is aged. Define the customers' payment problems and resolve any differences as quickly as possible.

Pay close attention to customers' complaints which might be used as a reason for delaying payment. If a complaint is justified, propose an agreement or an adjustment that will expedite payment.

Follow up closely on new promises for payment of delinquent accounts. Try to obtain payment on the promised date or request a valid reason for the new delay. Judgment must be exercised, of course, in just how hard you press for collection.

Make sure that credit is warranted before you grant it.

Is All This Record Keeping Too Much for You?

It seems complicated. And it really is complicated for anyone not used to or interested in keeping detailed records of business transactions. However, the simplest of one-man businesses needs some method of determining its status, just as does the giant corporation. It isn't solely a matter of observing the laws, statutes, regulations, and tax rules concerning the operation of a business. It's a matter, very much, of knowing where you've been, and where you're at, so that you can monitor your progress against plan and take corrective actions where the need is indicated. If keeping the books is more than you bargained for, hire a part-time or full-time bookkeeper. *Record your progress or you may have none.*

4

Organize Your Growth

THE successful small-business manager regularly reviews plans, his objectives, the direction in which his venture is moving, and the legal form or structure of his firm. It is valid and appropriate to wonder if the business would be better off set up differently. What is best: the sole proprietorship, general partnership, limited partnership, or corporation? Should it continue as it is operating? Is it worthwhile to make a change? If starting a new business venture, which is the best legal form?

Of course, the final answers to legal form questions and the specific steps in forming the structure must be handled by an attorney. However, very often the small-business manager may not really know what questions to ask an attorney. Too, some questions are actually in the realm of response by a certified public accountant.

This chapter is intended to provide a comprehensive understanding of the basic features and differences among the several choices available. This understanding will provoke questions with respect to individual situations that can then be referred to the appropriate channels for response.

Take, as an example, the fictional Albert Jones. Accumulating financial resources from his own savings plus a loan on his personal assets, he started a small air-conditioning service business. He was diligent, had the appropriate background in service work, worked long hours, and had the personal equation that gave him good references that lead to very gratifying business growth. Now, Al has a modern, efficient, well-equipped factory with 73 employees, and a sales volume of $735,000 a year.

Al started as sole owner of the business and enjoyed the ability to make independent decisions. He did not spend too much time thinking about the structure of his company. There was no need to change; things were going so well. But, Al was also intelligent and practical enough to listen when his accountant made suggestions. And, eventually, the accountant brought up the subject of status quo versus the effects of legal reorganization. Statistics on the tax effects were among the most influential arguments presented by the accountant.

It seemed that last year the firm made a net profit of $37,500. Despite his personal and family expenses, Al paid personal income taxes on the entire $37,500 profit. After subtracting $4,000 for exemptions and valid deductions, he reported an income of $33,500, on which he paid $9,290 in taxes. If Al's company had been a corporation reporting its income on the calendar year basis and he had taken a salary on the order of $17,000, his tax bill would have been:

Personal income tax on $17,000 salary (less $4,000
exemptions and deductions) = $2,510
Corporate taxes on net profit (after salary) of $20,500
= $5,330

Thus, if the company had been incorporated, Al would have saved $1,450 in taxes just for last year. This seems worthwhile, especially since there would have been no objection from the Internal Revenue Service to a $17,000 salary for the president of a business Al operated. Comparable executives get as much or more for services they actually perform in Al's industry.

Al went to his lawyer armed with a good reason for investigating the legal details of making a change in his company's organizational structure. His attorney reviewed with him the three main choices, the three principal kinds of business forms, starting with his present sole ownership.

Proprietorship, or sole ownership, is the easiest kind of business to start or to terminate. It needs no government approval beyond local or state licenses. Taxation is simple, the same as for personal income taxes; all profits are considered personal income of the owner. And, the owner is personally liable for all debts, taxes, and commitments which are applicable to the company's business affairs.

Partnership is among the simplest forms for two or more people to begin and end a business venture. Each partner personally shares the liabilities as well as the profits of the business. Taxes are calculated as individual, personal income equal to the profits of the business.

Corporation is the most formal of all structures. A corporation is an entity which operates under state laws. The life of the corporation is continuous, unlike the proprietorship or partnership, which terminates on the resignation or death of one or more of the participants. The corporation alone, not the executives or officers or stockholders, is liable for the debts and taxes of the business. Profits of the corporation are taxed separately from the salaries and other earnings of the owners and managers.

Other types of legal structures can be created, such as syndicates, joint stock companies, Massachusetts trusts, and pools. These are highly specialized, quite rare, and therefore omitted from our review.

Risk and Business Form

An investor in a business venture always is concerned about the risk he takes, not just in the amount of his financial investment but with respect to personal, legal liabilities for debts and taxes. In all legal structures, regardless of type and form, creditors are entitled to be paid out of assets of the business before any equity capital can be withdrawn. In cases of business failure, the ultimate risk, the extent to which owners or investors can be compelled to meet creditors' claims out of their own pockets, varies with the type of organization. Be aware, too, that in a strict sense any one to whom back wages are owed is a preferred creditor. Residual assets of a defunct business must be used first to meet salaries earned but not yet paid.

A *single proprietor* is personally liable for all debts of his business operations. He cannot restrict his liability in any way. Any personal assets can be applied by law to meeting his business debts and taxes.

Each member of a *general partnership* is fully responsible for all debts of his business, without regard to the actual amount of his investment in the business. It is technically quite easy to establish a general partnership. An agreement is reached among the partners. Although it is customary to formalize the arrangement in writing, an oral agreement or actions which imply an agreement can be just as effective.

A *limited partnership* requires a written agreement filed with the state government. This becomes a contract among the general partners who operate the business and the limited partners who participate as investors without actively participating in management. This contract enables limits to be placed on the liabilities of the limited partners, equal to just the amount of their investments. A limited partner must have actually invested in the business, using cash or other tangible property. Services may not be used as the limited partner's investment. Each state has rules and regulations governing the business conduct of a limited partnership. Failure to observe them can cause the business to be considered as a general partnership, thereby making all partners equally liable for the company's debts and taxes.

A *corporation* as a business structure offers the least risk of personal assets. Creditors can apply legal pressures to force payment of their claims only to the extent of the company's assets. Investors are shareholders. While a shareholder may lose the money he invested in the company, he cannot be required to contribute additional support out of his own personal assets to meet the corporation's debts and taxes.

A corporation is considerably more complicated to form than the other types of structures described. It must rigidly follow the legal procedures established by the state in which it is set up. Articles of incorporation must be prepared and filed with the designated state official. Corporate officers are named and identified by titles. Taxes and filing fees must be paid to the state. Also, if the business is based in a state other than the state of incorporation, additional taxes and fees may be required by the state in which it is headquartered. Various official meetings of the officers or board of directors of the corporation must be held periodically, and a book of minutes of the meetings must be maintained.

Life of the Business Form

Single proprietorships and partnerships have no time limit set by law on the life of the agreements or of the business structure. They are considered impermanent, dependent on the capacity of the active owners to perform their functions. Illness can disrupt the operation of a sole proprietor's business, disturb the efficiency of a partnership. Death or permanent disability of the sole proprietor or of a general partner terminates the agreements. Withdrawal of a partner from a two-man partnership ends the agreement.

Corporations have a separate, continuous life of their own. Withdrawal, disability, or death of an active officer or stockholder of the firm does not necessarily shut down the operation, does not automatically terminate the corporate structure. Certificates of stock which represent investment and ownership in the business may be transferred from one person to another without affecting the legal structure of the corporation.

It is certainly worthwhile to spend time with your accountant to determine the form of business organization best suited to your specific needs. Remember, too, that changes in the economics of your business will be occurring throughout its life. Make periodic reviews of where you are, and of where you intend to go. With some clear thoughts on your next move, meet with your legal counsel and take action. Or, confirm that no change is needed.

5

Successful Recruiting and Training

A sole proprietorship type of business operation does not necessarily mean a one-man business. In fact, from a legal viewpoint, there is no limit to the number of employees any business owner may have working with him. Of course, there *is* the pragmatism of it all.

Determining Personnel Needs

There is an optimum number of employees for any business venture. As the business grows from the minimum size of the one-man business, the proprietor begins to think, "I used to be able to do everything, but now there just aren't enough hours in the week. I'm held down because I have to do everything myself." Thus, he begins to think of adding help, full time or part time.

Hiring a helper can relieve the key man of time-consuming detail work and enable him to spend his time and energies in more productive directions, working with or selling to customers, or manufacturing his product, or providing his billable services. Yet, many small businessmen are reluctant to take on an employee.

Perhaps it is reluctance based on lack of knowledge of how to recruit and train new help. Perhaps it is based on fear of acquiring new problems with new employees. The desire is to keep it simple. But, finding, hiring, and training new people need not be a chore and, if pursued properly, need not present unmanageable problems.

The reluctance to hire is not exclusive to the one-man operator. Many managers resist adding to the staff for the same reasons. Because they allow this reluctance, these fears, to cloud their judgment, they never gain time or the freedom from details that enables them to plan properly, make decisions, and control.

Do You Really Need Another Employee?

Examine the present operation. Can you realign duties or reassign your present people so that all tasks are fulfilled? Are some kinds of work no longer necessary?

Overtime may provide an economical solution. Consider the possibility of offering present employees an opportunity to earn extra income for extra hours of work. Keep in mind, though, that they must not be allowed to slow down during regular hours to make overtime work. Prepare a written list of tasks or output expected from the overtime employees so that you and they can measure the effectiveness and the real economic values of the extra pay.

Temporary help is another approach that is often used to break bottlenecks. It may be practical to reduce expensive overtime, with its added costs of fringe benefits, by hiring the services of part-time labor, employees of a contract service organization. This may be useful if a person is needed for a short time, for vacation relief, for replacement during an illness, or to help with a temporary increase in work load. There are many agencies that offer experienced people on a limited time basis. These agencies take care of all the employment obligations required by government regulations, insurance, taxes, and any reporting requirements. The flat fee charged takes care of everything and, of course, is entirely charged out as a valid business expense.

Hiring another employee may be the only answer. Perhaps the added tasks extend over so long a period of time that it is not economical to pay overtime or to bring in a contract employee. It may be better to hire a new employee, add to the staff. A new person often brings new ideas, fresh thoughts that stimulate the present staff. The new employee can also provide a cushion in the case of illness or other unexpected absences of other employees. A trial period with a new employee is a practical way to learn whether or not an added hire is essential.

Finding the New Employee

Before the search begins for a new employee, time must be taken to determine what the job is and what qualifications are needed to perform it. Too often a new employee is taken on without a clear understanding of what is expected of him. In such cases it is very probable that a conflict will arise from the fact that the employee thinks one thing is expected of him and his supervisor has something completely different in mind. Too often such experiences end in a quitting or firing episode. Tempers and time are lost.

Write down the job duties. Describe exactly what the job is all about. Note to whom the employee reports. If the job is supervisory, also note who reports to him. Large companies minimize the confusion, loss of time, and the potential loss of good people by requiring a written *job description* before a new hire can be effected. Sample forms for job descriptions and help in filling them out are usually available without charge at state employment development offices.

Look inside your own firm. Don't overlook the capabilities of the existing staff. Promoting from within is an excellent way to grow the organization because the people are known to you, and it motivates others to work harder and more effectively when they see the opportunity for reward. Employees gain much satisfaction from knowing they were at least considered, even if they don't get the promotion, and will cooperate more fully with anyone brought in from the outside under these conditions.

Let your key employees know that you are looking outside for additions to your staff. Making them aware of your plans will eliminate embarrassment. Invite them to help in the search. Perhaps they have friends with a set of skills that closely matches the needs.

Make use of the no-charge services of the state employment development service. Often they will also pretest potential clerical employees, which can save you time and make selection easier.

Employment agencies offer another source. They charge fees, regulated by local or state laws, for their services. Job applicants usually pay the fee. In some cases the employer pays the fee, depending on the level of skills and whether or not the skills are in short supply and an extra inducement is needed to effect the hire.

Trade schools are a source of trained apprentices. Local high schools and colleges, too, often maintain lists of people looking for part-time or full-time work. Or, they will often post the announcement of a job opportunity where interested students can be made aware of it.

Hire Right—Train Right

When the new employee reports for work, he should not be allowed to fend for himself. Impressions obtained and given the first day or week are long-lasting. Set up specific on-the-job training procedures. Be specific in the instructions given to the new employee. For example, do not hand him a pencil and a bunch of cards with the instruction, "Take inventory." He should be shown; it should be demonstrated exactly what is meant and just how the inventory is taken.

Some managers orient a new employee by putting him under the guidance of a senior employee in whom they have confidence. It flatters the senior and assures that a proper introduction will be made to the methods of operation. Follow up regularly to see how the new employee is learning the work.

And let the new person know how well, or how poorly, he or she is doing. Set up a known probationary period, and at the end, review with the employee your evaluation of work performance. This is the time when the new employee will be most receptive to inputs from the supervisor, when the critique will be received as constructive. Everyone benefits.

Building an Asset: The Service Technician

Most owner-managers of distributor-service organizations have to train their technical servicemen in their own ways of doing business. Usually there are two aspects to this period of training or learning. One is the technical knowledge and application skills related to the hardware or products. The other is customer relations, the proper presentation of the organization's image to the end user of the product. Often a service technician or engineer is heavily skilled in one area and needs special assistance in the other.

A technician may know the product's technical idiosyncracies inside out and be able to trouble-shoot and repair very speedily, yet he may have an adverse personal effect on the customer. Or, the converse may be true. The customers may love him but he may seldom do a professional repair job, free from callbacks. The man who is bad on both counts is best transferred out of the shop. The ideal man is a rare one, of course. But since the serviceman is responsible for the effectiveness and profitability of the service operation, make every effort to realize the ideal. There are some very specific. things that can be done.

"Training" is an unpleasant word. Nobody likes to be trained, but almost everybody likes to learn. Perhaps that's the basis for the colorful colloquialism "You've got to learn 'em." So, to enable servicemen to excel at both aspects of their jobs, you've got to learn 'em real good, for better profits and long-term security.

A senior employee who has not proven himself capable of performing well or adequately in technical and personal aspects presents special problems. In the interest of clarity and making our points, we will deal with new hires or additions to the staff. A careful reading of this chapter will also provide suggestions on how to upgrade performance or make the senior man more adequate to the job and the organization's objectives.

Regardless of previous experience or training, the new technical service employee requires a period of adjustment to your way of doing business. The speed and success of the adjustment depends to a great extent on the guidance given him. Some shop managers don't use any system and provide no guidance because "He's supposed to know the work." One can see that this is naive and may represent the thinking of a manager who doesn't plan, who goes from crisis to crisis taking things as they come. Another type of shop manager carries his "plan" in his head; however, such a plan is too often neglected in the daily hustle and bustle of running the shop. In either case both the new employee and the business, not to mention the customer, suffer.

Before an owner-manager can help a new employee to adjust to his way of getting a job done, he has to decide what kind of or level of learning is needed by the individual. It is unrealistic to assume that, because the employee has experience with similar hardware, he automatically is able to service yours speedily and dependably. He may not have dealt with your special kind of customer either. Conclusions must be reached as to exactly what kind of technical training will be made available to him and what shortcomings in customer relations must be reworked.

The best way to decide the type of learning experience

the new man needs is in steps, starting with the initial interview, reference check, and what professional personnel managers call "orientation." The orientation should be received the first day on the job.

Be specific in informing the new employee about his duties, responsibilities, compensation; company objectives and image; and the usual details about working hours and fringe benefits. The next step is explaining in detail just what is expected of him, the job to be done.

Share a job description with the employee so that you *both* have a clear understanding of the expectations. The next step is showing him how you expect the work to be performed. One of your senior employees or you should go through it with him in person.

Emphasize the importance of doing a good job and taking pride in the finished work. These first few days and weeks are among the most important in developing the technician. How he is supervised, handled, or managed during this orientation period could determine his value, make him an asset or a liability, a contributor to growth and profit or a destructive expense item. A large part of the responsibility rests with the owner-manager.

When it is apparent that the new technician has learned how to do the job, whether in applying his technical skills or in customer handling, only occasional supervision should be necessary. But, periodically, the owner-manager should monitor specific skills to assure himself that the technician's self-discipline is being sustained.

Make sure you point out the kinds of problems you expect the technician to bring to your attention when he is out on his own. Encourage him to communicate with you. Keep the lines open. However, as he becomes more experienced and you develop greater mutual confidence, his checking with you will decrease in frequency.

In following through, do not forget to give, periodically, a person-to-person appraisal of his performance. Twice a year is a good frequency for such a constructive discussion. You will want to check on and discuss the quantity and quality of his work, his knowledge of the hardware, his work habits, and his ability to fit into the team. This helps the technician, or any employee for that matter, know where he stands. Also, it helps you determine the extent of any additional learning courses that should be explored in an effort to make him still more valuable by increasing his technical skills and knowledge.

Consider very seriously the unique benefits that come from having technicians, service engineers, even field sales engineers attend courses of instruction offered by equipment manufacturers. In the long run, many of them are well worth the short time the technician is out of service and in school. If you chose the man well and have followed through, enabling him to upgrade his craftsmanship and knowledge, he has to become one of the most valuable of the company's assets.

Employee Laws

You are familiar with employee laws if you are already employing people. However, if the firm is just getting ready to take on its first employee, you should know certain facts about the laws that apply.

Federal and state laws concerning employees are designed to provide minimum standards of wages, minimum standards of working conditions, and maximum limitations on the use of employees, for protection of their health and welfare. Such laws are designed not so much to restrict or regulate the small-business owner as to protect the employee.

The Fair Labor Standards Act sets minimum wages and overtime pay and puts some limitations on hours. Whether your firm is covered by the Act depends on your situation.

The Act regulates firms that engage in interstate commerce, but many states have set similar wage minimums for firms operating within the state. Some also require overtime pay for work beyond 40 hours a week.

The Social Security Act requires you to share in the cost of providing minimum retirement benefits for your employees. The tax rate calls for you to pay a specific percent of the employee's salary. Each employee contributes a similar amount up to a maximum dollar amount per year.

Federal income tax legislation requires the deduction of the income tax from the employees' pay according to their dependency status. The employer is obligated to collect the proper amount and turn it over to the government. Dependency status forms (W-4) for employees to fill out are obtained from any office of the Internal Revenue Service.

Each quarter, reports on the amount of Social Security (FICA) tax and income tax deducted from employees' wages have to be filed.

You should also keep in mind that any moneys deducted from wages should be specifically authorized by the employee in writing. The only exception allowed by most states is garnishment or wage assignments issued by a court. In the case of the federal government, the only exception is the Social Security tax.

An Equal Pay Act was passed by Congress, but many states have similar legislation. These laws require that men and women receive equal pay if they are performing the same work.

The states are also active in supplementing the federal standards and setting their own as well. Employee laws vary from state to state.

Nearly every state restricts the number of hours and types of work minors may do. For example, most states prohibit minors from working more than eight hours a day, operating moving machinery, or engaging in occupations injurious to their health. Usually, a minor must obtain a work permit through his local school system.

Be especially careful about the work assigned to minors. In many instances, the employer who works minors in violation of state requirements may be subject to a severe penalty in the event of their injury or illness.

Many states require that employees be granted a day of

rest each week and that there be a suitable space and reasonable time afforded for rest or lunch periods.

If any unusual employment conditions exist in your business, be sure you are observing your state laws. If in doubt, check with the state department of labor, usually located in the state capital.

Most states require regular payment of wages due an employee. As a rule, payday is seven to fifteen days after the work period ends. In some situations you may pay employees monthly. However, monthly payment is usually reserved for employees who are exempt from overtime requirements.

All states require workmen's compensation coverage for employees so that they may have medical and hospital treatment if they are hurt at work or become ill because of their work. Workmen's compensation also insures that employees get a portion of their regular income while recovering. Generally, this coverage can be provided through a state insurance fund or, in many cases, through your own insurance broker.

Information about state disability insurance can be obtained from the department of labor in your state.

The firm also pays the cost of unemployment insurance protection for its employees. Such insurance provides unemployment benefits for employees if they are laid off and are actively seeking other suitable work. Details about this tax, if you have never employed anyone, can be obtained from the state employment service office.

Complex But Not Difficult

If all the other businesses in your field, including your nearest competitor, can do it, so can you! In fact, you have no choice but to do all the things the city, county, state, and federal governments require of you as the owner or manager of a business. The small business and the large business alike have to keep the records, pay the taxes, and file the reports.

Yes, as the small business grows larger, there is more demand for pursuing peripheral details. It cannot be done in a haphazard way. Planning and controlling are continuous management functions. Growth is among the normal ambitions of the manager of the business. Organize, develop an orderly manner of growth, so that the fruits of labor may be maximized.

PART TWO

accounting,
finance,
and
management

6

Money Has
Its Own Language

SOME terms used in the financial world are reasonably precise. We know exactly what they mean, and there is little room for error or misinterpretation. Then there are terms whose meanings are thought to be known quite well but, at the same time, they are open to interpretation.

All is not confusion, however. There are standards related to the sources of data, the display of data, their interpretation and applications in the diagnosis and guidance of a business venture. The American Institute of Certified Public Accountants (AICPA) is among the recognized authorities which help avoid chaos by establishing standards of good practice in the language of money as related to business finance.

A practical vocabulary of business finance is essential to the successful small-business manager. There are basic words and accepted definitions with which the enlightened businessman should be familiar, whether they crop up in conversation with a customer, supplier, his accountant or bookkeeper, or with the bank's loan officer. For example:

Cash. Straightforward "coin of the realm," bills and coins in the cash register, petty cash box, or on deposit in the bank; tangible money within ready access for immediate payment of such things as salaries, loans, and accounts payable.

Accounts payable. Debts owed, usually stated in terms of money, by the company to suppliers of goods or services which were purchased or contracted for on open account or on a line of credit, and for which payment is due within the next 12 months.

Accounts receivable. Debts owed, usually stated in terms of money, to the company by others who bought its products or services and for which they have been invoiced with payment expected within the next 12 months.

Notes payable. Part or the whole of promissory notes which fall due within the next 12 months.

Notes receivable. Money owed to the business by those who signed notes promising payment for purchases on or before a specific date. The due date is usually expressed as a number of days or months following the date of the note itself.

Reserve for bad debt. The best estimate of the worst accounts receivable, the debts on the books which are least likely to be paid back. The "reserve" is an estimate which reflects the net value of losses which might occur from uncollectable accounts. These accounts might never pay up and therefore represent money that can't be depended on as income, even though they are legitimate debts.

Advances to employees. Company assets so listed when they include dollars which must be accounted for by the employees and returned to the company's cash account. Such items as travel or petty cash advances, loans, or salary advances are in this category of assets.

Cash forecast. A prediction of future cash requirements for operating the business. Based on a very realistic forecast of billable shipments, it can indicate what is most likely to happen, provide a guide to planning for growth (or retrenchment), project when borrowing may become necessary, and give an estimate of how much to seek from lenders. It is an appraisal of the amount of cash coming in and the amount to be paid out for a given period of activity.

Accounts receivable aging schedule. Segregates the amounts owed by each customer into time intervals of current, 30 days, 60 days, 90 days, and over 90 days past due. It tells how long it takes for the average customer to pay his bills and whether or not the credit policy is lax, gives an indication of what to expect from whom in bad debts, becomes a basis for making cash forecasts, and aids in establishing credit limits on specific customers on the basis of history of payments.

Mortgages payable. That portion of the principal of a mortgage which is to be liquidated during the next 12-month period.

Prepaid expenses. Money paid in advance for such items as rent and insurance. Their benefits are to be consumed in the forthcoming 12-month period. These are also known as *deferred charges.*

Inventory. Items which have been accumulated in the acquisition or manufacture of a product, or in the fulfillment of a service, and which are to become part of the product or be expended in the completion of the service. It includes raw or unfinished materials, materials in various stages of completion and known as work in process (WIP), and finished goods ready for sale. Valuation of inventory is normally stated at original cost, market value, or current replacement cost, whichever is lowest. This practice is approved because it minimizes the possibility of overstating earnings and assets.

Marketable securities. Temporary investment of idle cash in stocks, bonds, or U.S. government securities in order to earn dividends and interest. The word "temporary" is important here because the money is intended to work on a short-term basis and be readily accessible on relatively short notice. Such securities must be readily marketable, or convertible to cash, and subject to minimal price fluctuations.

Accrued expenses. Expenses for goods or services which

have already been received but not yet paid for.

Gross sales. The total invoiced price of merchandise or services sold, after deducting discounts but before deducting returns and allowances.

Returns. Merchandise returned with permission for credit or refund.

Allowances. Extra discounts allowed, usually to customers who place large orders.

Net sales. Gross sales less returns and allowances.

Cost of sales. A combination of the following costs: materials acquired in the manufacturing process, freight-in, direct labor utilized in the manufacture of the product or in performing the services, and a portion of overhead (the cost of operating the production or service facility).

Gross profit. Net sales less the cost of sales.

Operating profit. Gross profit minus operating expenses.

Operating expenses. The costs necessary to allow the business to perform its functions, that is, the costs of necessary services or labor, whether purchased or on the payroll, plus allocated overhead.

Net profit (or loss). Operating profit *plus* "other income" *minus* "other expenses."

Other income. Profit and income to the business not resulting from the sale of merchandise or services. Typical examples include recovery of bad debts which had been previously written off, gain on sales of assets, interest received on notes receivable, and earned cash discounts.

Other expenses. Expenses incurred by the business but not as a direct result of sale of inventory or of services. Examples are losses on sales of assets, interest on debts, and cash discounts allowed to customers.

Provisions for taxes. Money earmarked to pay taxes which are based on net profits. Make certain in calculating cash available for continued operations that you consider profits *after* taxes.

Long-term investments. Purchases of marketable securities or other devices with the intention of earning income beyond the next 12 months through interest, dividends, or appreciation (as with real estate).

Fixed assets. Long-life physical resources which are used over and over again in the conduct of the business. They are expected to have a service life in excess of one year and are reported at cost on the balance sheet. Items included in this category are:

Automobiles	Delivery equipment	Tools
Buildings	Leasehold improvements	Land
Machinery	Real estate	Property
Fixtures	Furniture	

Reserve for depreciation. The amount deducted from fixed assets to assure accurate calculations of net worth. The same amount is added to expenses, reducing profits and providing a resource for replacing the assets when the end of their lifetime of usefulness has arrived.

With the exception of land, most fixed assets have a limited economic life or value. The cost of an asset is spread over its expected useful life and within guidelines of the Internal Revenue Service. Depreciation should be calculated so that it is equitably allocated to the periods during which services are obtained from the use of the asset. The method suited to your needs is best determined by an accountant familiar with your business structure.

Other assets. Long-term investments, prepaid expenses and deferred charges, advances to employees, and loans given.

Current assets. Items that can be converted to cash during the normal course of business and within the next 12 months. The more common current assets are cash, accounts and notes receivable, inventories, and short-term investments.

Current liabilities. Debts which are due for payment within the next 12 months or less. The more common current liabilities are accounts and notes payable, mortgages payable, and accrued expenses.

Long-term liabilities. Debts or other financial obligations due to be paid after the next 12-month business cycle is completed. The 12-month cycle is the period immediately following the date of the company's balance sheet.

Balance sheet. The financial statement which represents a summary of a company's financial resources on a given date. It is usually prepared for specific purposes such as to demonstrate viability to money-lending agencies or other prospective creditors, or to prospective investors.

P&L statement. A financial statement of the profits or losses resulting from all the business transactions over a period of time. It can be prepared for a time interval as short as a day or a week but it is more practicable to cover a month of operations and to include a summary of year-to-date activities. It tells the score.

If you are to be a successful business manager, you have no choice but to become fluent in money-talk. It is not optional; it is mandatory.

The business manager must be able to communicate with his accountant, financial officers of his supplier companies, his bookkeeper, creditors, investors, and his bank. It is difficult to imagine a business manager generating confidence while talking to the loan officer of a bank if he does not understand questions about assets, liabilities, and cash forecasts. Similarly, how can one expect a supplier to grant a significant open account status to a company managed by a person who doesn't understand the standard, universally accepted but special language of the financial community, or who can't describe his company's position in that language?

The meek may one day inherit the earth. But the naive among them will not know what to do with their valuable inheritance.

7

Break Through
the Profit Barrier

THE major objective of all the time, energy, money, and emotion dedicated to operating the business is to generate a net profit. How much profit is actually required may be a matter of personal ambition or need. Naturally, there are practical limitations on the amount of profit a given set of financial, material, and human resources can generate. The prudent manager, who has set his objectives and time scale realistically, has established the plan and the controls that give maximum assurance that profits will be generated.

One of the reasons for generating profits is to create additional cash for the purchase of assets that can enable the business to grow with a vigor that will offer an opportunity to generate still more profits. It is a cascading or regenerative process of money, properly managed, begetting more money.

Profits derived from operations provide the means for meeting extraordinary expenses, for purchasing new inventories, for acquiring more production equipment and space in which to house it, for promoting added sales volume, for penetrating new markets, for developing new products, and, of course, for raising the personal standard of living. Losses from business operations are counter to the usual objectives of the economic organization of a free enterprise system. Regardless of what definition one may use, profit is the motivating force in the business of anyone reading this book.

Profit is the positive, upswinging side of a business curve. *Loss* is the negative, downward slope of the curve. At some point between profit and loss there is a finite position known as *break-even*. Obviously, therefore, the term "break-even" refers to a point in business operations and financial analysis where neither a profit nor a loss is sustained; the total of costs exactly equals the sales volume, both expressed in dollars.

While break-even may be described as being better than a loss, one must not lose sight of the objective, which is to make a measured profit. In determining the break-even point of business operations, either mathematically or graphically, the manager uses a tool for decision making and for solving many complicated business problems concerning the relationships of price, volume, costs, income, and profit. This tool is called "break-even analysis."

Advantages of Break-Even Analysis

Break-even analysis provides a flexible set of income and expense projections under assumed conditions of magnitude and helps point the way to alternative approaches to growth and problem solving. To develop a realistic approach to our own objective for success, we must understand clearly the influences which specific increases or decreases in sales volume and operating expenses will have on our profit goals. Break-even analysis enables the business manager to study the interactions of volume, selling prices, costs, and product mix.

Through the application of break-even analysis to budgeting, expenses can be more closely controlled. Just how much can we afford in such items as payroll, rent, and equipment? How do we measure these things so that timing of cash outlays can be accurately determined? Break-even analysis permits a realistic determination of the cost-related aspects of selling price, because it can be used to illustrate the effects of alternative pricing proposals integrated with variations in unit volume.

The graphic presentation of break-even analysis provides an easy-to-read report which summarizes data contained in various income statements. It illustrates the effects of alternative proposals when changes or increases of capital expenditures are involved. It is characteristic that where there is opportunity for profit, there is risk for loss. Similarly, the break-even chart or graph offers unusual benefits; but there are limitations.

Limitations of Break-Even Analysis

Because the development of meaningful break-even points is related to the reliability of the source data, one must be certain of the validity of the inputs to the computations. If you have been maintaining accurate records of operating dollars, costs, and income, you are on the right road to deriving the benefits of break-even analysis. If you are knowledgeable or have dependable information about market conditions and the relationships between various selling prices and the effects on sales volume, you are in a position to develop the assumptions that tilt the usefulness of the break-even analysis in your favor.

You have to know your costs. These costs must be segregated into two classifications: fixed and variable. Unfortunately, fixed expenses have the habit of not remaining fixed, and variable expenses refuse to vary in direct proportion to sales volume. Also, break-even analysis usually ignores the cost of maintaining inventories.

In order to continue, we will conclude that there is a good, dependable "fix" on costs and how they are affected by changes in the size of the business. Also, we will assume that you are an accomplished marketeer or have access to dependable marketing skills.

Break-even analysis is a means for measuring profit probabilities using assumptions rather than definite facts. One of the assumptions is an oversimplification of a complex situation. It requires that selling price be held constant over the entire range of each projection. Changes in prices, product mixes, and channels of distribution can throw such an assumption out of line with reality.

In addition, break-even analysis uses manufacturing expenses along with selling and administrative expenses in its computation. The inclusion of manufacturing expenses assumes that production and sales volume remain approximately identical. So, when inventory is being built up or cut down, one may calculate sales to be at a break-even point, while in reality, a profit or loss may be realized under accounting procedures. Competition and the dynamic conditions of economy often cause shifts that upset the assumption of static conditions. Therefore, when calculating profit, loss, and break-even points, it is worthwhile to develop *sets of projections* based on different *sets of assumptions*.

Despite the long list of limitations, the advantages of break-even analysis significantly outweigh its limitations.

Costs

The word "costs" has many meanings, and care must be taken to make sure that its application to a given situation is understood.

Variable costs are those that vary with volume. Make more product so that more can be shipped and invoiced, and the costs for labor and material directly applicable to the product will increase. Such labor and materials are referred to as direct costs or expenses; they are directly identifiable and chargeable to a specific project.

Fixed costs are those which can be expected to remain constant despite changes in sales volume. These include executive, general, and administrative salaries and benefits, interest charges, rent or mortgage payments, equipment leases or depreciation on owned equipment that cannot be classified as direct, and engineering, technical support, or product development expenses.

Semivariable costs are yet another category; however, for purposes of calculating or projecting break-even points, they must be redefined as either fixed or variable costs. Semivariable costs tend to fluctuate but not necessarily in direct relationship to production or sales. Typical of this category are advertising and sales promotion, advanced research not directly chargeable to a product, and market research expenses. Experience and judgment serve as the basis for the individual determination of the reclassification from semivariable to fixed or variable.

Sources of data are found in historical records of operations. It is practical to use profit-and-loss statements of past performance. This approach is ordinarily precise enough to serve the purpose. The break-even point established with the profit-and-loss statement as the source of data can be used as a guide in setting policies relating to changes in pricing and in product, as an aid in determining maximum cost levels that can be reasonably tolerated, and as a timetable for planning future expansion of plant or facilities.

Creating the Break-Even Chart

For this exercise we will create a simplified profit-and-loss statement for the ABC Company.

Year Ending December 31, 19XX
($ millions)

Total sales		$ 8.2
Cost of goods sold	$ 5.3	
Selling expenses	1.2	
General and administrative costs	0.8	
Total costs	$ 7.3	
Profit (before taxes)		$ 0.9

In order to prepare the chart from the basic data derived from the P&L statement, costs or expenses must be separated into fixed and variable categories.

	($ millions)	
Element	Fixed expense	Variable expense
Direct labor		$ 1.6
Direct materials		2.4
Factory burden (overhead)	$ 0.9	0.4
Selling expenses	0.5	0.7
General and administrative costs	0.6	0.2
Totals	$ 2.0	$ 5.3

Now we begin to make assumptions which enable us to place reference points on the chart. Our first assumption is that the fixed expenses will remain or be controlled to remain at the same level for all forecasts of sales volume. Our basic chart is shown in Figure 3.

Note that the vertical axis of the chart is calibrated in dollars. The horizontal axis, or the base line, may be calibrated in units or, as in Figure 3, in percent of plant capacity. Increments of 10 percent, up to the maximum of 100 percent, are used in referring to plant capacity.

With the ABC Company as our model, a line is drawn from the $2.0 point on the vertical axis parallel to the base line. This is labeled "fixed expenses." Our assumption is, again, that fixed expenses will not change.

The total expenses figure does increase with volume or capacity as more labor and materials are directly applied to production. This data is applied to the chart, starting at the same point as the fixed expenses on the assumption that even if the factory produced zero units or operated at zero percent of its capacity, the fixed expenses would still apply. Variable costs are "on top of" fixed costs and become the line labeled "total expenses."

Next, a line is drawn diagonally from the zero point, the conjunction of the vertical and horizontal axes, to the $8.2

Figure 3. Break-even chart.

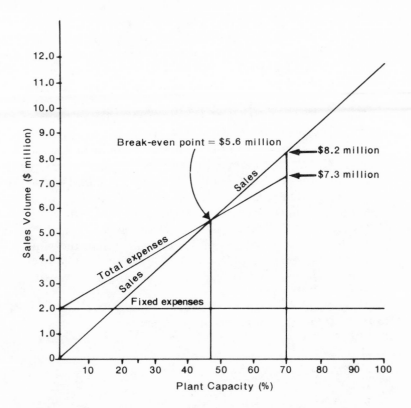

million sales level. In the example of the ABC Company it is known that sales of $8.2 million are generated at 70 percent of plant capacity.

The break-even point is identified as the conjunction of the "sales line" and the "total expense" line. The ABC Company would have to produce approximately $5.6 million in sales, or utilize 48 percent of plant capacity, to break even. At a lower volume of sales, the indicators report a loss position in operation. At a volume of more than $5.6 million and utilization above 48 percent of plant capacity, a profit is indicated.

Dynamic Input Break-Even Chart

The break-even chart in Figure 3 illustrates the assumptions of nonvarying fixed expenses and straight-line variable expenses for all levels of production or sales volume. It is possible to depict graphically the effects on break-even, profit, and loss by charting changes in expenses as plant output is increased or decreased.

The dynamic input break-even chart is shown in Figure 4. The assumption used is that pricing of the product varies as the volume of sales increases, accounting for the tapering off at the high end of the sales line as plant capacity or output increases. Note that the total expenses tend to rise at the high end, appearing to meet sales dollars. Also, it is apparent from this chart that an effort is being made to calculate changes in fixed and variable expenses as plant capacity is adjusted upward. This is closer to reality than the simplified break-even chart of Figure 3. One can see that there is a considerable area in plant capacity, approximately 35 to 55

Figure 4. Dynamic input break-even chart.

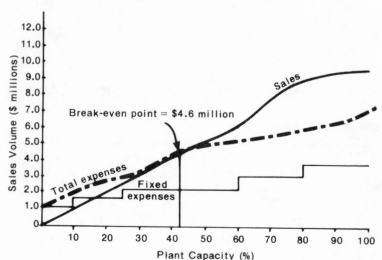

percent, where the difference between profit and loss is very small. Break-even is at 42 percent, but minor variations in expenses, slippage in controls, can move the profit-and-loss statement to one side or the other of break-even. It appears, too, that major profits can be realized, by any measurement method, with shipments at 70 to 90 percent of plant capacity.

Needless to say, Figure 4 is the more valuable, probably the more valid, approach to deriving the benefits of break-even charting. However, it does require a good knowledge of costs at all levels of production, marketing, general, and administrative operations. Once again, a good set of books—records of the business operations, income, and expenses—is invaluable.

Using Break-Even Information

Break-even charts can be very useful in making decisions to purchase new capital equipment. What effect does such a purchase have on fixed expenses? On variable expenses? Does one rise while the other falls? What is the net impact on total expenses? If the reduction in variable expenses is offset by an increase in fixed expenses, which include amortization and maintenance costs, the break-even point may rise to cause a reduction in profits for a given volume of sales.

Profits and losses can be figured from the break-even chart simply by measuring the vertical distance between the sales line and the expenses line at any given plant capacity. This vertical distance is then compared with the vertical sales-volume line to arrive at a conversion to dollars gained or lost.

Recognize the fact that break-even charts are not a panacea for operating losses. Nor are they a guarantor of profits. They assume a set of conditions which are subject to change. However, if they are updated to reflect current cost data, they serve admirably as a management tool—an indicator of where control may be required in general areas of the operations and a valid information source for planning the near-term future.

8

Reduce Costs
and Increase Profits

IN Chapter 7 it was demonstrated that increased profits may be derived from a decrease in costs. Also, it was demonstrated graphically that increased profits may come, but not always, from an increase in sales volume. Without exception, the successful small-business manager plans, monitors, and controls both costs and sales to maximize the net profit.

No area, department, or section of the business operation is exempt from his scrutiny. The successful, entrepreneurial manager seems to be everywhere, to have knowledge about every aspect of the business he manages. If he doesn't have a number or a fact at the tip of his tongue, he knows exactly where to lay the tip of his finger in the files. He is a veritable dynamo of activity as he quickly looks at the bottom line of the P&L statement and then pores through the supporting data above the line. Of course, he is studying the variances in cost and sales, comparing them with budgets or plans, making basic management decisions to implement programs for sales-income increases and cost reductions. It is the latter effort we will deal with at this time, leaving the former for a later chapter.

What do you suppose is the basic tool for developing a manageable cost reduction program? Records, of course. Unless adequate records are kept under an appropriate accounting system, there can be no basis for ascertaining and analyzing costs.

What Is Cost Reduction?

Cost reduction is a technique for getting more value or greater return on each dollar spent in business operations. Cost reduction is not simply a slashing of any and all expenses without method, rhyme, or sense. The successful business manager understands the nature of expenses and how they interrelate with sales, inventories, cost of goods sold, gross profits, and net profits.

Cost reduction turned around means profit improvement. Cost reduction does not mean only the reduction of specific expenses. Remember that a big sales volume does not necessarily produce a big profit. Too many managers become frustrated and perplexed when, despite their professional and effective efforts to build sales volume, the P&L statement reveals a decreased net profit.

Analyze the Expense Dollars

There are numerous, specific areas that deserve review, even if only to confirm that expense levels are proper or are at the irreducible level. If yours is a retail store, look at the payroll expense. Establish measures of productivity for each sales clerk paid to sell merchandise. Consider training sales clerks to make multiple sales, do more than say, "Will that be all, sir?" Train them to be aware of opportunities for add-on sales. To use an old example, whenever a customer buys a toothbrush, it is appropriate to suggest a toothpaste purchase. This builds sales volume per unit of sales effort. Increased productivity results in greater profit, the actual objective of cost reduction. Is this cost reduction? Yes, it is, in that the cost per sale is reduced as the productivity of the selling-expense dollar is increased.

Continue to bear in mind that slashing budgets and laying off people are to be used as a last resort. Why as a last resort? Should the business turnaround and profitability be restored to the point where expansion is practical, start-up costs known as the "learning curve" can be a mighty expensive process as new employees are brought in, or those who were laid off are rehired, or budgets are restored. It has been said that American industry is on a perpetual learning curve. There is a tendency to respond to each crisis with dramatic, easy-to-do budget cuts and massive layoffs.

Records Continue to Be Important

Before it can be determined whether cutting expenses will increase profits, information is needed about operations. Once again, this information can be obtained only through an adequate record keeping system. Intelligent action requires current information. An adequate record keeping system is one that is accurate and current.

Major attention must be focused on variable expense items. These are more readily controllable.

Reduce Distribution Costs

Distribution cost analysis helps classify accounts as profitable or unprofitable, or it helps determine the proportion of time and expense required to service customers. Six basic company records are used: (1) names and locations of customers, (2) types of businesses of customers, (3) number of individual orders from each customer in a given period of time, (4) total sales volume received from each customer in a given period of time, (5) total sales and gross profits on each product in the company's catalog, and (6) expense items such as warehousing, transportation, packing, shipping, advertising, salaries plus commissions of salesmen, salesmen's travel expenses, bad debts, and insurance.

With these facts at hand it is possible to shift emphasis from unprofitable to profitable accounts. It may prove desirable to spend more face-to-face selling time with profitable accounts, using telephone and direct mail contacts for the less profitable accounts. This increases the productivity of the sales force and the associated expense dollars. Again, increasing the return on the sales-dollar investment is a positive form of cost reduction. It may be practical to rearrange sales routes, consolidate or revise territorial boundaries, or transfer salesmen from one district to another as account analysis reveals the needs for special talents or unique sales skills.

In examining distribution costs, the business manager can determine through past experience whether it is more desirable to lease or purchase additional equipment to improve merchandise handling at the warehouse, with an eye to reducing losses through breakage or misrouting of shipments.

In most enterprises, a small proportion of the territories, customers, transactions, or products are responsible for the overwhelming bulk of the profit dollars. A careful examination of well-kept records can help determine whether a large proportion of the money spent in the marketing effort is producing a small return.

Analyze the Marketing Costs

In the typical small business, selling, advertising, and similar marketing efforts are expended in proportion to the number of customers, historic sales volume, and number of orders, instead of in proportion to potential sales. This means there is a distorted spreading of marketing efforts, judging by results which, as was pointed out, state that a majority of the business volume comes from a minority of the customers or products.

There are several reasons for this "distortion." Many business managers do not track their marketing efforts by account, and by time and costs required to service them individually. It is not easy to do such a cost analysis, but without it there can be no specific control or direction of selling efforts toward the profitable customers or products. Experience shows that, frequently, a large number of sales made by a firm are unprofitable even though the business as a whole shows a profit. When the business manager becomes aware of such facts in specific terms, he is often faced with a decision of whether or not to keep an unprofitable account on the books or a money-losing product in the line. It is true that, even when the numbers staring hard and cold at the manager say "drop it," there may be extenuating circumstances that resist the action. Factors of judgment must always be taken into account, or cost reduction efforts concentrated elsewhere.

It is not unusual for any business, large or small, to discover that 80 to 90 percent of its sales are being generated by only 15 to 20 percent of its accounts. This means that 80 percent or better of its marketing efforts are being wasted.

This does not mean that 80 to 85 percent of its accounts should be dropped. Who would give up 10 to 20 percent of his sales volume as easily as that? It does mean that an analysis of the marketing expense is called for, that the marketing and distribution methods are in need of close examination.

Order-getting costs are incurred in advance of the sale or the shipment of merchandise that enables an invoice to be cut and an account payable added to the company's assets. Order-getting costs vary not in response to sales volume, as do factory costs, but in anticipation of sales volume, according to decisions made by management. In one case, costs *may* vary in accordance with sales volume. In the other case costs *do* vary with sales volume.

Everyone Must Participate

Cost control authority and responsibility must be delegated. It does not matter whether the responsible person is a senior vice president or a line supervisor. What does matter very much is that the cost centers of the business firm must be defined, segregated, and responsibility for each one delegated to a specific person. Carefully define each person's responsibility and duties relative to keeping costs down. An expense budget is to be considered the *maximum* level of expenditure allowed to produce a planned result. The aim is to spend less than the budgeted amounts. If it can be proven that the budget is unrealistic, a new number must be agreed upon, and that becomes the budget.

Having definite functional subdivisions, divisions, departments, or sections makes improved control possible because (1) the manager of the business is enabled to devote more of his time to overall planning, and (2) the ingenuity of the individual division, department, or section managers is stimulated; their personalities become involved and motivated. The accounting system for budgets should be set up to report actual costs versus budgeted costs in terms of organizational responsibility.

Plan for Progress

Planning pertains to all companies regardless of size. Planning provides the only sound foundation for cost control. The most dangerous costs are those which build up through lack of supervision of the *opportunities to spend:* Discounts may be missed through oversight. Long-distance telephone calls may be made where letters would have sufficed. Careless handling may cause damage to materials. Damaged materials may be discarded without investigation for possible reclamation. Travel may be done first class when tourist would have been acceptable. The highest priced hotels and finest restaurants may be used without a view toward economizing.

One should not expect the employee or the company officer traveling on business to live poorly while on the road. On the other hand, a temporary and drastic change upward in the standard of living can add heavily to the cost of operations. In the case of the traveling marketing or sales man, it has a significant and measurable impact on the productivity of the marketing budget.

It is essential to have a specific plan of budget control. The main purposes in drawing up a written plan of operations budgets are to make certain that all participants are aware of and agree to the budget dollars and the areas to which they are assigned by plan, and to provide a control document which may be the monthly report of budget, actuals and variances from budget.

Developing the Expense Budget

It is assumed that a sales forecast or budget has been developed and has become part of the records of the operations. Estimate the costs that are expected to be incurred in meeting the sales forecasts. As in Figure 5, list the fixed and variable costs separately by month. It will be useful to display the comparable data for the same month of the previous year. A separate sheet is developed for each cost center. A composite sheet is prepared for the combined centers, the total operation.

The column headed "Last Year" carries the actuals, not the budget as it was at the time. This column provides a snapshot look at the directions taken by individual entries, increases or decreases by item. Some companies add another column to permit apples-to-apples types of measurement. A percentage is placed in the column alongside each item's dollar report. This presents the item as a percent of sales or shipments for the month. This way, one avoids confusion over changes in product mixes or other effects that impact on the pure dollars. Each dollar statement relates to the same reference point, shipments.

Figure 5. Data sheet for developing the expense budget.

					INITIALS	DATE
Department Name_____				PREPARED BY		
Expense-Control Report for_____ 19___				APPROVED BY		

Expense Items	(1) Last year actual same month	(2) Current budget	(3) Actuals for month	(4) Variance from budget	(5) Actuals as a % of sales	(6)
Fixed Expenses	$ %					
Salaries						
Rent						
Insurance						
Taxes						
Utilities						
Depreciation						
Advertising						
Sales promotion						
Public relations						
Travel						
Entertainment						
Manufacturing						
Supplies						
G & A						
Subtotal						
Variable Expenses						
Commissions						
Materials						
Direct labor						
Manufacturing						
Travel						
Entertainment						
G & A						
Subtotal						
Total Expenses						

In skimming the monthly expense report, one sees the percentage figure first, draws a rapid comparison, and begins to zero in on the variances from history and the variances from present budget. A budget has significance only when the plan is realistic. The actual technique of the columnar display of information may be a matter of personal management technique and preference, within the guidelines of good accounting practice. The information shown in Figure 5 can be separated into two or more sheets. For example, one sheet might be used to display current budget versus actuals, another might provide the historic comparisons, and a third might be used to display historic versus present data as a percentage of sales, a valuable indicator of whether the profit picture is getting brighter or dimmer. The objective of this collection and display of data is to allow the development of specific programs for applying controls to specific elements of cost.

Cost reduction is a tool for profit improvement programs, called "PIP" in large companies. This is one technique of large company management that is of immense value to all companies, without regard to size.

9

Depreciate Your Assets

WITH few exceptions, from the first day a capital asset is acquired it begins to lose value. The everyday example is in the purchase of a car. As soon as title passes from the dealer to the buyer and the car is driven off the lot, the car is considered to be a used vehicle and its resale value drops by a measureable amount of dollars. Each year its value drops still more.

So, too, with many of the capital assets of a business: The value depreciates each year until the individual asset is deemed to be worth only its residual content, junk metal, for example, in the case of machinery. This continuous loss represents one of the costs of doing business. Within limits, it is a controllable cost.

The cost of the asset is properly chargeable as an expense over its useful life translated into a finite number of accounting periods. The Accounting Principles Board of the American Institute of Certified Public Accountants offers a definition of the gradual conversion of fixed assets into expense, or *depreciation:*

The cost of a productive facility is one of the costs of the service it renders during its useful economic life. Generally accepted accounting principles require that its cost be spread over the expected useful life of the facility in such a way as to allocate it as equitably as possible to the periods during which services are obtained from the use of the facility. This procedure is known as depreciation accounting, a system of accounting which aims to distribute the cost or other basic value of tangible capital assets, less salvage (if any), over the estimated useful life of the unit (which may be a group of assets) in a systematic and rational manner. It is a process of allocation, not of valuation.

All goods and services consumed by a business during an accounting period are expenses, and depreciation is considered to be such an expense. The useful life of a capital asset is limited for two major reasons: *deterioration,* the process of physical exhaustion, and *obsolescence,* the loss of usefulness or the accelerated termination of life caused by the development of improved equipment or new processes, or by other factors not necessarily related to the physical condition of the asset. Depreciation relates to both causes. No distinction is made for accounting purposes. The distinction may be made for management information only.

"Depreciation" is not a synonym for "wear and tear." For example, suppose the business purchases a pickup truck for $6,300 and, after operating it for 100,000 miles, sells it for $300. The truck depreciated $6,000 in value up to the time of disposal. The *depreciation cost,* per mile, was 6 cents. The *cost of maintenance,* repair, oil, and fuel was expensed as part of the *cost of operations* in the year in which the repair or maintenance charge was paid. The moneys disbursed in keeping the truck in good repair maintained the value of the asset, reduced its rate of depreciation.

The life of most capital items cannot be measured conveniently in units of use, or output, or production. To use the same example of the truck, it is not practical or meaningful to translate its cost in terms of how many pieces of merchandise or materials it hauled. Its usefulness must be related to time. time.

The truck had been operated for three years. Thus it depreciated, on a straight-line basis, at the rate of $2,000 per year. It might have been operated for six years and then sold for a scrap value of $50. Then the depreciation would have been $1,041.67 per year. Or, it might have been so well maintained and in such excellent repair that a dealer might have allowed $975 in trade-in value against the purchase of a new truck. In this case, the depreciation would be the original purchase price less the recovery value, divided by the number of years of operation ($6,300 − $975 = $5,325 ÷ 6 = $887.50 per year).

Cost of depreciation depends in part on policy within the guidelines of the Internal Revenue Service, on how well the asset is maintained, and on how long it is held.

Depreciation Methods

There are three accepted methods of calculating dollar depreciation of a capital asset: straight-line, double declining balance, and years-digits. The last two are considered accelerated methods of depreciation, the effect of whose calculations is to write off approximately two-thirds of the cost in half the asset's estimated life.

Figure 6 illustrates the three methods for comparison, for a machine costing $10,000 with an estimated life of ten years and no salvage value.

The straight-line method considers that the asset depreciates at a uniform rate, in equal amounts for each year of its useful life. For example, if a machine is estimated to have a ten-year life, one-tenth its cost is taken as depreciation in the first year, one-tenth in the second year, and so on, until the end of the tenth year, when the residual value is estimated to be at zero dollars.

The double declining balance method applies the depreciation to the book value of the asset at the beginning of the year, rather than to the original cost of the asset. "Book value" is the cost less total depreciation accumulated up to

Figure 6. Comparison of depreciation methods.

YEAR	STRAIGHT-LINE (10)		DECLINING BALANCE (20)		YEARS-DIGITS	
	BOOK VALUE	ANNUAL DEPRECIATION	BOOK VALUE	ANNUAL DEPRECIATION	BOOK VALUE	ANNUAL DEPRECIATION
Starting	$ 10,000	$ —	$ 10,000	$ —	$ 10,000	$ —
First	9,000	1,000	8,000	2,000	8,181.80	1,818.20
Second	8,000	1,000	6,400	1,600	6,545.40	1,636.40
Third	7,000	1,000	5,120	1,280	5,090.90	1,454.50
Fourth	6,000	1,000	4,096	1,024	3,818.20	1,272.70
Fifth	5,000	1,000	3,276.80	819.20	2,727.30	1,090.90
Sixth	4,000	1,000	2,621.40	655.40	1,818.20	909.10
Seventh	3,000	1,000	2,097.10	524.30	1,090.90	727.30
Eighth	2,000	1,000	1,677.70	419.40	545.40	545.50
Ninth	1,000	1,000	1,342.20	335.50	181.80	363.60
Tenth	—	1,000	1,073.80	268.40	—	181.80
Eleventh	—	—	859	214.80	—	—
Twelfth	—	—	687.20*	171.80	—	—
		$ 10,000		$ 9,312.80*		$ 10,000.00

*Note: Under the declining balance method, depreciation continues until the asset is disposed of or until the book value declines to the salvage value. In the later years of an asset's life, it is not unusual for a company to switch from declining balance to straight-line methods and write off the entire cost in a specified number of years. This is an accounting method acceptable to the IRS and to auditors.

that time. The tax law permits the company to take double the rate allowed under the straight-line method, thus the "double declining balance."

The years-digits method develops a ratio which is the sum of the digits of the years—1 + 2 + 3, and so on, up to the number of years *n*, which is the estimated useful life of the asset. The annual depreciation rate each year is a fraction in which the denominator is the sum of these digits and the numerator is *n* for the first year, *n minus 1* for the second year, *n minus 2* for the third year, and so on. Assume an example in which the estimated life (*n*) of a machine is ten years. The sum of the digits, 1 + 2 + 3 + 4 + 5 + 6 + 7 + 8 + 9 + 10, is 55. In the first year, depreciation would be 10/55 of the cost; in the second year, 9/55, and so on.

Use of Judgment

In order to determine the depreciation expense for an accounting period, each fixed asset must be reviewed and certain judgments or estimates must be made:

What is the *service, or useful, life* of the asset? What is the period of time over which the asset will be useful to the company?

What is the *salvage or resale value* of the asset at the end of its useful life? The salvage or resale value of the asset plus the amount depreciated cannot be greater than the cost of acquiring the asset. Should the total become greater, a profit must be reported.

What *method* of depreciation should be used to allocate a portion of the acquisition cost to each of the accounting periods of the asset's useful life?

Depreciation Guidelines, published by the Internal Revenue Service, is the most widely used basis for estimating service life of assets. This publication gives estimates for specific categories of machinery and equipment. It covers many items, from office equipment to factories and office buildings.

Special attention is called to the use of the word "guidelines." The life terms of the assets described by the IRS are not mandatory. If the company believes that a specific unit of assets will become obsolete or deteriorate at a faster rate than suggested in the *Guidelines*, the company should use the more advantageous estimate. An example is provided by the manufacture of semiconductor devices, an industry faced with such continuously changing techniques and technology that a unit of sophisticated processing equipment might become virtually obsolete within a year or two of acquisition and installation. The determination of depreciation method or allocation to accounting periods is best achieved by specific examples in consultation with the company's accountants or tax specialists and the IRS.

Deterioration

When a piece of equipment is purchased—a delivery truck, a milling machine, a display case, a cash register, or what have you—the company buys an expense item. The expense is in the using up of the equipment through wear and tear—deterioration—as a result of use, or even nonuse. Deterioration cannot be stopped; it can only be slowed down by doing preventive maintenance to minimize failures and wear, and by making repairs when needed. These are expenses of operating the business. If equipment is neglected, neither maintained nor repaired, the deterioration and the depreciation are accelerated. On the other hand, the business firm usually has no control over *obsolescence*, which may cause a sudden termination of useful life or measurably shorten it.

Depreciation Affects Income

Whether you use the equipment to produce sales or let it stand idle, the value of the asset declines. For tax purposes, depreciation starts when an asset is acquired and ends when it is disposed of. The decrease in value is a periodic business expense and must be subtracted from current income, as is any other expense, when calculating profit and loss for a specific period of business time.

Depreciation through obsolescence is among the most difficult estimates for a businessman to make. One is scarcely able to determine accurately when the dynamics of technology will create a new production tool, one that must be acquired in replacement of existing equipment if the company is to remain competitive. Because of this obsolescence factor, many businesses obtain consent of the IRS to a fast write-off. The advantage is in timing only, not in the amount of depreciation allowed.

Depreciation Affects Assets

Just as the dollar depreciation must be deducted from income, the same amount must be deducted from assets. The deductions may be accumulated in a separate reserve-for-depreciation account. When the reserve-for-depreciation account plus the salvage value of the equipment equals the total cost of the equipment plus installation expenses, the asset is defined as "fully depreciated." No further depreciation expense is charged for the specific asset item.

Selling an Asset

What happens when an asset is sold? You may get less than its remaining or estimated market value, or you may get more. If you receive less than the remaining value, the difference is a reduction in income for the year in which the sale of asset is made. This may result in a loss for the year. Provided certain conditions are met, that loss can be deducted for tax purposes in the three years prior or in the five years following the sale. These conditions are subject to changes in tax regulations published by the IRS, or new court rulings.

If the amount received from the sale of the asset is more than the remaining market value, it is considered a gain which must be added to the income for the current year. It is a pure *capital gain* and affects taxable income on that basis.

Depreciation does not represent money that can be used to purchase new or additional assets. Depreciation is not money. The money owned by the business is shown only in the cash account. No one really knows how long an asset will last or what its residual value will be at the end of its useful life. The depreciation figure is therefore an estimate based on experience and judgment.

Effects of Inflation

During a period of rising prices, no practicable formula for depreciation will permit recovery of full replacement cost over the life of an asset. It is difficult, almost impossible, to predict accurately the price rises or the price for a replacement asset of the future. Also, assets are often replaced at the end of life by an item that is different in type, size, or capacity. Despite an apparent inequity, the original cost plus installation remains as the basis of depreciation for tax purposes. The time will most certainly come when the asset must be replaced because of deterioration or obsolescence; therefore, the *cost of replacement* rather than the *cost of acquisition* must become a consideration in pricing current products.

While there are certainly many variables that are considered in pricing a product for resale, including competitive, economic, and current cost factors, the prudent business manager plans ahead for the day of reckoning when cash will be needed for replacement of assets which have a direct effect on his ability to compete successfully.

10

Danger Signals
in Cost Estimating

IN a previous chapter the importance of *cost reduction* was described in relation to *profit improvement*. In proceeding toward an organized program of cost reduction the manager acquires much specific detail about every aspect of operations, labor, time, and materials. There is an extremely important added benefit derived from this detail, these records of costs. It is exceptionally valuable in determining the prices for bids on contract work. These cost details are essential to accurate bidding, one of the keys to operating profitably in a competitive industry.

Working up a correct bid, one that will not only win the award but also be profitable on completion, requires time, patience, careful attention to detail, dependable source data, and ingenuity. By following certain steps a small businessman can ease the burden, reduce the risk of loss, and enhance the probability for profit. These steps include (1) understanding the job specification, (2) knowing material, labor, and equipment costs, (3) evaluating and properly allocating overhead, (4) determining the job duration, (5) building employee morale and enthusiasm for the job, and (6) avoiding complacency.

Understand the Job Specification

Don't make a single move until every line and word of the job specification, invitation to bid, or solicitation is thoroughly understood. If the specification has been written by the customer or his agent, do not hesitate to make contact and clarify any ambiguities or omissions from the written specification. If there are conditions, characteristics, or features that your specialists feel are not realistic or practicable, discuss a revision of the specification with the people who offered the invitation, or who made the solicitation.

It is not unusual for a set of specifications to be withdrawn for rewrite, or an amendment to be published. If you are unsuccessful in obtaining a revision that your specialists feel is essential to the fulfillment of the terms of the specification, and you still feel there may be some benefit to making a bid—such as assuring that your firm's name will stay on the bidder's list—do so, but take exception in writing to the particular specification under challenge.

If you do not want to bid, for whatever reason (it may be unprofitable, or the time limit may be unachievable because of work already on the books), respond in writing to indicate that your company is not bidding on this invitation but would like to remain on the bidder's list for future solicitations. It is possible, too, that you may not want to bid because of the customer's financial weakness. It is not essential in open bidding to reveal the reason for not making a bid. Individual judgment alone determines just how much one discloses about one's actions.

Know Material, Labor, Equipment Costs

Assume the job specification is understood, any exceptions have been resolved, and you are ready to begin working up the bid price. First estimate the cost of direct material, labor, and equipment. Do not omit the cost of any equipment that may have to be leased for this specific job. Such a lease becomes a direct cost. If the equipment time is to be shared with other jobs, only that portion of the time allocated to each job is charged directly.

It is valuable, in the interest of accuracy, to prepare a cost detail sheet for each bid and to keep a copy with a duplicate of the bid response in a file under the control of the individual responsible for coordinating all internal affairs related to bid actions.

Material costs should be calculated at realistic price levels. If existing inventories are used, standard costs may apply. However, if additional materials must be acquired, current market prices must be considered. Be certain to include freight-in and any other applicable acquisition costs, such as duty and import taxes.

Labor costs must be calculated accurately for the job. It may be dangerous to use average labor costs. If time studies have been made on operations related to the job, use this data in developing direct labor costs. List the tasks of the job, whether it is a service or a product or a combination that is being offered. Each task or phase of the job will require a measurable number of man-hours or man-days. Multiply the man-time by the hourly labor rate for the task; add payroll taxes, workmen's compensation, vacations, insurance, and any other benefits your company provides. If on-site work is required that takes men away from the plant, remember the costs of travel time, and per diem out-of-pocket charges for transportation, food, and lodging wherever and to whomever they may apply.

Equipment costs will depend on whether the equipment is owned or rented. Cost of operation should be broken down to dollars per hour, day, week, or month for each piece of equipment applicable to the contract. If the equipment is owned, depreciation may be allocated to the contract as well.

Evaluate, Allocate Overhead

Overhead is a group of continuing costs which cannot in their entirety be charged to one particular task, service, or product. Overhead includes such things as warehouse and storage space, insurance, taxes, rent, telephone, office personnel, and general management salaries and benefits. The general level of overhead expenses may be determined from the business records.

Assume items identified as "overhead" last year totaled $240,000 on a gross sales volume of $1,600,000. On a percentage basis, overhead was 15 percent of gross sales. A ratio or a percentage factor for overhead makes it easier from an accounting standpoint to prorate such expenses to short-term jobs, specific tasks, services, or products. The use of percentages must be made with good judgment, taking into account factors of inflation and any other impacts on general expenses. Once again, good record keeping is mandatory.

Overhead expenses may be included in the exercise of developing the bid price in one of several ways:

□ Add a standard percentage to direct costs. (This practice may apply to costing any product, service, or job contract.)

□ Add to direct costs an amount that represents a carefully worked out evaluation of the specific management costs to be consumed by the contract.

□ Add to direct costs the best estimate of what overhead costs may be incurred and what costs the contract will tolerate. This is a matter of judgment rather than science.

Parochially adding a flat percentage of direct costs to all bids can be quite risky. However, if overhead charges drive the bid price too high and out of line with competition, the award may be lost. On the other hand, if too little is charged for overhead in an effort to win the award by "beating out competition," profits may disappear and business life may become hazardous.

Determine Job Duration

Direct costs do not vary with the length of time it takes to complete a job, normally. In practice, however, this is not always true. Poor coordination, late arrivals of materials, or high rejects of subcontracted supplies can make a job take longer to complete than had been originally planned in costing the job. This is always a risk in bidding a contract. It is very important to recognize this risk, try to estimate the negative probabilities, and plug them into your time-to-completion section of the bid response.

High Morale Can Be Profitable

Good relations with contractors, vendors, and suppliers are motivational influences that can make the difference between success and failure in meeting cost and time targets in completing an awarded contract. When relationships are positive, all conditions are go. When relationships are bad, it is sometimes amazing how many things can go wrong with shipments, deliveries, and quality. And, it can be terribly frustrating as well as unprofitable. Be aware, too, of the need for support from your banker, insurance people, public agencies, trade associations, trade unions, and, naturally, your employees.

Beware of Complacency

It's dangerous to think you've got it made because the contract was awarded to your firm. Guard against psychological impulses such as can come from the feeling that "I've done this kind of job before and can do it with my eyes shut." Maybe you can do it with your "eyes shut"—but don't! Even though you've calculated this kind of bid invitation before, do it as though it were brand new to you. Calculate your costs and your profit under *current* conditions. They could be quite different than they were last time you did the same sort of job.

Don't panic when competition seems to win several job awards in a row, bidding below your price. Recheck your figures at once to reassure yourself that your company's bid was realistic, with no fat. It is entirely possible your competitors are tying themselves up with unprofitable contracts, and that's not the way to play the winner's game.

Every bid should generate profit on completion of the contract and collection of payment. It should be calculated to generate profit. Submitting a break-even bid, trading dollars, is business brinkmanship. The temptation may be great to try to win an award just to cover costs and overhead. However, too often the unexpected comes along, increases the job costs, and turns the situation into a loss—just when you can least afford it. Be aware of all the risks, no matter how small, and price the bid response to cover contingencies and still produce a profit.

When the award is made to you, develop a budget for costs in detail. Prepare a timetable, too, for each phase of the contract. Then, record and monitor all actuals, comparing them periodically with the budget. This will indicate when and where to take corrective action to assure success.

11

Are You Pricing
for Profit?

IT is fundamental that the selling price for a product
or service should maximize the difference between income
and costs. In order to do this one must be competent or
skilled at two types of estimates: the *emotion-demand factor*
which forecasts the units sold at various price levels, and the
effects on variable costs caused by incremental or decre-
mental changes in units of product or service delivered to the
customers.

Scientific techniques can be used in determining variable costs in relation to volume; however, there is probably
more art than science involved in forecasting how a market
will respond to specific changes in selling prices. Who can
accurately estimate what quantities will be sold at one price,
let alone at all possible prices?

The challenge of such a forecast is so great that few
companies attempt to estimate the emotion-demand curve.
Relatively few managers have ever seen one. It takes cour-
age to present such a schedule to the top management of a

corporation. It requires supernatural talent to develop an emotion-demand forecast that will prove to be consistently accurate in practice. Of course, the rescue comes from the fact that there is no opportunity to practice an emotion-demand schedule within the same time period as it is forecast. The forecaster uses as much science as is possible in developing the selling price and then brings art into play to estimate demand or volume.

An overeager attempt to maximize the difference between cost and selling price is unworkable. This attempt to maximize is also unpopularly referred to as "gouging," "profiteering," and "charging all the traffic will bear." It not only has an unethical sound; it also promises a rapid loss of customers and an early demise for the company that prices in this way.

Fortunately, most responsible business managers use the concepts of *satisfactory profit* or *satisfactory return on investment.* Another term for "satisfactory profit" is "reasonable profit" for the type of business in which the company is engaged. And this leads us to the specific pricing techniques employed by those who strive for long-term profits and continued growth in competitive environments.

Merchandise and Product Pricing

Manufacturers of hardware or high-technology products, whose list prices or selling prices are published for all potential customers to see, do not face the highly dynamic set of conditions of the storefront or the retail operation. These manufacturers usually do not have severe pricing problems. Often, a market price exists as a result of competitive industry-wide conditions. There is no reason why the product should be sold for a lower price. But customers will not pay a higher price. In many industries there are no price leaders, and the price level is determined by the amount the buyer will pay. This is the *market price.* There is no need for calculating selling prices; they are obvious. The market price is what is charged.

Full-cost pricing is the usual practice for a company that does have the problem of determining its selling price. Simply expressed, full-cost pricing computes the full cost of the product or service and adds to this a margin of profit. This margin of profit is developed mathematically, either as a percentage of the total of fixed and variable costs or as a percentage of the return on the investment involved in making the product or in rendering the service.

This appears to be a rather mechanical approach and, because of this, has a certain appeal. It simplifies the decision-making process for a company with a complex catalog or with different lines of merchandise, products, or services. Add up the costs, add on the percentage, and there is the price. Supporters of this approach to pricing point to the protection built into this system. If one has taken all costs into consideration and a relative profit is put on top of these costs, a profit must result the moment a sale is made and paid for.

However, as that last sentence clearly indicates, one of the keys to making a profit is that a sale must be made. This is like the famous old recipe for making fish chowder, which begins, "First, catch a fish." Often, a rigid, inflexible approach to pricing, one that is based on strict use of a formula, leads to prices that are somewhat higher than competition is charging for similar output. As a result, sales forecasts may not be realized.

It is appropriate, however, to start with facts which include full costs and reasonable profit or return on investment. The result of this calculation should be considered an *approximation* of the price. The real world requires compromise. This takes into account the strength of competition, the necessity of fitting the price into customary price lines (such as those of a store with the slogan "Nothing over $9.95"), and other marketing considerations. As a result, products in the catalog, merchandise on the racks, and services sold may produce profit margins and returns on investments that vary from one item to the other. The important factor lies in the bottom line of the profit-and-loss statement for an accounting period which shows whether or not, *on the average,* goals for the business activity were missed, met, or exceeded.

Flexible pricing is the approach used by merchants in retailing activities. They consider a range of influences in setting prices. In a supermarket, for example, a record may be kept of the sales activity for a can of fruit selling at 41 cents. An estimate is made of how many more cans could be sold at a unit price of 39 cents. If the increase in sales is enough to offset the price reduction, a special may be announced. Consideration is also given to the reverse situation; perhaps raising the price of a fast-moving piece of merchandise will not affect the unit sales volume appreciably. The unit profit increases and, if the estimates prove to be accurate, the profit for the sales period is increased.

Flexible pricing is often used to "meet competition." When a store drops its price on certain merchandise, it may become essential for the store down the street to meet competition by lowering its price in order to continue to move the merchandise into the hands of the buyers. The merchant who uses flexible pricing to meet competition usually increases the price of another item to offset the decreased unit profit of the item that has been price-reduced. In these examples, the effect of price changes can be felt immediately. Unlike the situation in heavy industry, customer reactions to price changes are immediate in most retail operations. Readjustments can be made rapidly to assure continued trade.

Flexible markup pricing is a common practice in retailing, used to protect profits or at least to assure recovery of costs. A "floor" is established on the minimum selling price for each item, and prices are not permitted to drop below this level. From this floor the merchant adjusts his markups to meet changes in consumer demand or competitive actions, protecting himself from pricing his merchandise too low.

Going rate pricing is an approach used by some businesses which cannot (because of the nature of the business) accurately track costs. They do not ignore costs in their pricing, but more emphasis is placed on market conditions and consumer demand. A garden nursery is a clear example of this situation. Costs are difficult to assess with accuracy because of the time it may take for plantings to mature and because of the variable effects of weather on the yield. Markup from cost has little meaning in this situation. The manager of such a business must be very much aware of the market condition in order to establish selling prices.

Another example is found in the radio and television repair shop. It is usual practice to charge standard prices for several categories of service calls or shop work, without regard to time put on each job. If the prices are competitive and the service technicians are competent, the unit profit will necessarily be low on some jobs, high on others, and the average profit will prove satisfactory. A markup is not used, nor are prices based on individual costs.

Gross margin pricing is sometimes used by merchants. The price is determined on the basis of wholesale rather than full costs. A markup is added as a percentage of the wholesale cost. For example, a jewelry store may determine that some items are fast movers, either because of their popularity or because of prevailing competitive low prices, and may add a markup of 50 percent over the wholesale price. On items which are slower-moving or subject to less competition, a 100 percent markup is commonly used.

Still another simplified approach to pricing adopted by some small firms is to follow the list of resale price suggestions of their wholesale suppliers. In such cases, management usually pays considerable attention to other costs and operating expenses in an effort to sustain profits and does not participate in competitive price-cutting practices.

Problems in Pricing Services

When a customer purchases a unit of merchandise or a product, the price is clearly stated. Something tangible is acquired by the buyer, and he can usually see and evaluate the benefit derived. However, when a service is purchased, the customer generally is aware only of the expenditure of a certain amount of labor or the results of that labor. For example, when a radio or a television set has been repaired, the set owner sees only the return of his own merchandise for which he has been charged a service fee. He has no specific knowledge of the difficulties involved in restoring the unit's performance. Or when the customer purchases dry cleaning services for his suit, he receives what he originally gave, a suit. He may not be aware of the time expended in identifying the spots and stains, and the manual labor expended in removing them. Many customers tend to underestimate the value of services for which they pay. This is because of the invisible, nontangible, mysterious, and misunderstood nature of the service rendered.

With respect to cost of providing the services, the customer thinks only in terms of a fair wage for the labor required to provide the services. Rarely does he think of the time required by the service technician to learn his special skills, or of the service equipment, tools, and materials used; overhead, including insurance and rent; and a reasonable profit to make it all worthwhile.

For many years, prices for services have been rising at a more rapid rate than have the prices for goods. Part of the reason for that is that productivity for service labor has not developed as rapidly as that for manufactured goods, and the high labor cost involved in providing services causes prices to soar.

Despite the disparity in price rises, service businesses have been growing faster than the general economy. As our society becomes more affluent, a large proportion of disposable income is made available for services, as well as for products that require follow-on service. Also, retailers continue to add services to their activities. Stores offer decorating and installation services. Some stores offer insurance services, with large chains dealing in such high-priced items as automobile insurance and small independent bicycle dealers offering bicycle insurance. Many appliance dealers have found it promotes sales and provides extra income to offer out-of-warranty service to customers. Can you think of a new-car dealer who doesn't have his own service department? Think of all the rental businesses: cars, trailers, tools, formal clothes, home furnishings, medical aids, books, camping equipment, and so many more.

Pricing New Products and Services

In many companies the profit margin is expressed as a percentage of cost. Other companies compute the profit margin as a return on the assets employed in manufacturing or selling their products and services.

Assume, as an example, that a company manufactures two products, Model Q and Model R. Manufacturing cost for each is $12 per unit. At a markup of 50 percent of cost, the published selling price would be $18 for each unit. If 100,000 units of each product are sold, the total margin would be $600,000. Under return-on-asset pricing, the company would estimate the total dollar value of the assets employed in producing the two products. Assume this calculates to be $6,000,000, or $60 per unit, for Model Q and $2,000,000, or $20 a unit, for Model R. The company business plan calls for a 15 percent return on assets. Thus, the margin would be $9 for Model Q and $3 for Model R. If we follow this concept of pricing, the normal selling price for Model Q would be $21, and for Model R it would be $15. These prices produce the same total margin as a 50 percent markup on cost; however, allocations of cost of assets are more equitably made. Model Q's higher price reflects the fact that more assets are required to make a unit of Q than a unit of R.

Profit Margins

New products and services that are indeed novel, not merely someone else's design in a different wrapper, deserve special treatment to maximize profitability. Although no other supplier manufactures or markets quite the same thing, this distinctiveness is usually only temporary for this reason: As the new product or service catches on, competitors will scramble to take away the market by bringing out imitative substitutes. The speed with which the "new" loses its uniqueness depends on a number of factors, including the total sales potential, the investment required for rivals to manufacture and distribute the offering, the strength of patent protection, and the alertness and power of competitors.

Although competitive imitation is inevitable in a free enterprise system, the company that introduces a new product, or a new service, can use price as a means for slowing the speed with which the competitive responses are made available. Finding the right price is not easy. New items are hard to price accurately in a way that provides an optimum return, or assures full return on investment, and at the same time deters competition. For a truly new product, there is little past experience on which to draw, either for dollar or unit forecasts. Therefore, in setting a price you will want to keep three objectives in mind: (1) Get acceptance, (2) produce profits, and (3) maintain a strong market position in the face of growing competition.

The strategy in pricing comes to a choice between *skimming pricing* and *penetration pricing*. There are intermediate positions, of course, but the issue is clearer when only the two extremes are considered.

Skimming pricing. Some products or services represent a drastic departure from the accepted ways, the traditional methods, of performing a service or filling a demand. For these a strategy of high prices, coupled with large promotional expenditures in the early stages of market development, and lower prices at later stages, has frequently proven successful. This is known as a skimming pricing policy. There are four main reasons why this policy is attractive for new and highly distinctive products and services:

1. The quantity of the sales made is likely to be less affected by price in the early stages than it will be when the product or service is full-grown and competitive imitation has taken effect. These early stages form the period when pure salesmanship, rather than price, can have the greatest influence on sales.

2. A skimming pricing policy tempts the high-ticket buyers before it becomes necessary to penetrate the more price-sensitive markets in order to maintain unit sales. This means the seller can make more sales to buyers who are willing to pay a higher price for a novel situation and at the same time can acquire valuable experience useful later in approaching the larger mass markets with reduced prices.

3. This policy can be used as a technique for feeling out the demand. It is frequently fairly easy to start with a higher price which may be rejected by the market and reduce it later when the facts of the demand make themselves known. It is usually more difficult to set a low price at the start and then boost the price to cover unforeseen costs or to capitalize on underestimated popularity.

4. High prices will frequently produce a greater *dollar* volume of sales in the early stages of market development than will a policy of low initial prices. When this is the case, skimming prices will provide funds for financing expansion into the larger volume sectors of the market.

Penetration pricing. Of course, a skimming pricing policy is not always the best approach to a new offering. Although initial high prices may appear to safeguard profits during the early stages, they may also prevent quick sales to the many buyers upon whom you must rely to get into mass markets early. The alternative is to use low prices as an entering wedge to get into mass markets as quickly as possible. This is penetration pricing, and it is desirable under the following conditions:

1. When the product or service offered is highly sensitive to price, even in the early stage of introduction of the novelty.

2. When substantial economies can be achieved in unit cost of manufacturing and distribution by operating at a large volume.

3. When the product or service is fully expected to be faced by threats of strong competition very soon after introduction.

4. When there is no "sophisticated" market, a class of buyers who are willing to pay a higher price merely to possess the newest and latest, inferring it's the best.

Skimming pricing may be used at the inception; penetration pricing may be used to rescue the offering from a sudden death due to competitive maneuvers.

Making a decision about which way to go, while diminishing the dependence on luck, requires the marketer to have in-depth and accurate knowledge of the markets and the competition's strengths.

From a general strategic viewpoint, if the selling price is set low enough to begin with, the large competitor may not feel it worth his while to make a big investment in developing, manufacturing, and distribution for the promise of small profit margins. For this reason, low initial prices are often referred to as "stay out" prices. In any event, each new offering of a product or a service must be appraised on its own set of conditions: return on assets needed to meet company goals, best estimates of market acceptance, and competitive reactions. Because forecasting is a technique that combines experience, knowledge, and "guesstimating" (more politely referred to as "art and science in combination"), alternate plans should always become part of the master plan for pricing and distribution of new products and services.

Adding or dropping products, a continuing management decision, calls for a similar analysis. A new product is normally added to the line with expectations of producing a satisfactory return on investment. Existing products which produce poor returns on investments are usually replaced when neither price increases nor cost reductions can correct a marketing situation. However, there may be a good reason for following another course. The low-margin product may be retained in order to complement other products in the catalog, or because it creates profitable sales of accessory items and supplies, or because no better product may be in the offing.

Companies who expect to sell their products in significantly varying quantities to several different accounts may base their pricing on full costs. The Robinson-Patman Act prohibits differentials in the prices charged customers who compete in the same markets, unless these differentials make due allowances for differences in total costs as a result of differing methods or quantities ordered. It is important to be aware of the professional negotiating skills of the purchasing agents of large companies who tend to drive hard bargains before they agree to a purchase contract. Under the Act any other company, large or small, is entitled to the same price if the quantities and delivery methods and schedules are identical—unless it can be proved conclusively that total costs were different for each contract and that the different customers do not compete in the same marketplace. This is not easily nor usually proven with legal conviction.

Contribution pricing, a rationalization for pricing below normal margins, is sometimes used in a crisis. In normal times a company may refuse to accept an order at a price that will not generate a satisfactory profit or return on investment. If times are bad, an order may be accepted where differential, variable, or incremental costs are exceeded by the differential revenue obtained as a result of the sale. Such orders make some contribution to profit, sometimes described as a *contribution to overhead,* and the exceptional selling price is referred to as a *contribution price.* The differential costs are calculated as those costs that will be incurred if the order is accepted and that will not be incurred if it is not accepted.

Dumping, the practice of selling surplus quantities of a product in a selected marketing area at a low price, is a version of contribution pricing. Dumping may be in violation of the Robinson-Patman Act in domestic markets. There may be similar restraints in foreign countries.

Building a Price Image

Often one hears a company described as "high price" or at some other level related to price. There is a philosophical aspect of price as related to value. A shoddy product or an unsatisfactory service can be considered high at any price. This indicates that value is the key to an accurate description of the vendor. *The relationship between price and value* is really what establishes a company's image, name, and reputation.

There can be no doubt but that the best way to get a good reputation on price/value is to offer quality service or prime products at favorable prices that are competitive while allowing the realization of a reasonable profit.

Discounting has a legitimate place in the business world. One form of discounting practiced almost universally is the discount-for-cash incentive. Invoices may carry a notice such as "2/10, 1/20, net 30." This indicates that the purchaser who has been billed may deduct 2 percent from the invoice total if he pays within ten days of the date of the invoice, or 1 percent within twenty days; the due date for the net invoice is 30 days from the date of the invoice. This is an incentive offered to the purchaser to pay promptly and thereby improve the cash flow of the seller.

Discounts may be offered for quantity buys, or for cash on delivery of the merchandise. It is popular among merchandisers, manufacturers, and service organizations to offer special discounts, valid for a specific period of time, to encourage new customers to buy the item or try the service, or to bring old customers back one more time. Manufacturers of items sold through supermarkets and drugstores frequently use discount coupons ("10 cents off with this coupon on the purchase of . . .") to introduce or revitalize the sale of disposable items. Automobile service stations may offer special incentives in the form of "Free car wash with fill-up" or "Free oil filter with lube job and oil change."

The discount department store has become an institution that thrives on volume, rapid turnover, cash payments, and a low average profit margin. The success of such an operation requires careful supervision, purchasing in quantities that offer lowest costs, and skillful control of pricing. There are examples of large chains of discount operations that appear to be succeeding. And there are outstanding examples of failure or borderline existences.

Obviously, one should guard against liberally discounting too many services and products. It is desirable to discount only on offerings which will lead to further nondiscounted business, or in order to move overstocked or surplus items. The automobile industry historically discounts previous model-year cars each time a new model-year line is introduced.

People are willing to accept special discounts or on-sale low prices. However, they are usually suspicious of either the quality of the merchandise received or the service given. Therefore, whatever the pricing policy, advertise it in your market area. Explain it to your customers. A clear-cut statement of policy is good promotion. People like to know about the firm with which they do business. Establishing and promoting the pricing policy will help avoid later controversy or dissatisfaction by building confidence.

How to Handle Price Increases

In periods of rising costs—and who remembers a period when costs were not rising?—it becomes essential to meet increased labor and materials costs with a rise in selling prices that maintains a fair margin of profit. When a price rise must be implemented it becomes important that it be done without diminishing volume.

Customers want to know, indeed they have a right to know, why they must pay an increased price for the same product or service. As a consumer, you may have reacted to sudden price increases by changing suppliers because you considered the increases out of line—or, probably, because the reason for the increases was not made clear. One of the most inflammatory actions a manufacturer, a wholesaler, or a retailer can do to his customers is to raise prices suddenly, without prior notice.

"Prices subject to change without notice" is a legend printed at the bottom of many printed price sheets. However, this is a requirement imposed by the legal departments on the marketing departments of suppliers, especially in large businesses which are exceptionally sensitive to government and civilian suits. The intent is not to warn the reader of the potential for deliberate surprise price actions but to make it known that when a price has been published, put in writing so to speak, it may not be practicable for the supplier to see that updated price information is placed in the hands of all the readers.

Nobody welcomes a price increase; feelings are bound to be hurt and negative reactions stimulated. On the other hand, it may be too much to expect a buyer to remain calm if he discovers the price has been increased after he has placed the order and has taken delivery of the merchandise or the services.

Make certain customers know about a price increase; at least make them aware of the latest price without calling it "an increase." It is customary, not mandatory but just good business practice, for manufacturers and wholesalers to give 30-day notices of price increases to their active accounts. This gives the buyer an opportunity to purchase inventory at the original price so that he does not have to face his own customers with the prospect of a sudden price increase. Some buyers take advantage of such 30-day notices in order to maintain competitive prices in their own markets, at least for the short term.

A brief explanation of the reason for the price increase is usually given by the manufacturer, the wholesaler, and the wise retailer. Often, a simple statement of rising costs requiring the increase is all that is needed. Sometimes brief details of the costs that affect the pricing are described—labor, materials, freight, insurance, and so on. Giant increases are sure to bring about serious buyer resistance. It is better to make two relatively modest increases in prices over a time spread, rather than take one giant step.

Price wars are hazardous to business health! Wildly cutting prices in an effort to knock out a competitor usually causes suffering to both parties in the conflict. Few small businesses have the resources to survive a price war. Large businesses that compete against small ones by indiscriminately cutting prices in selected markets with selected products or services risk the wrath of federal regulations and are monitored closely by the Federal Trade Commission.

Complaints rising out of prices must be handled promptly. Delaying or avoiding settlement usually complicates the situation. Whether in person, by letter, or by telephone, make certain of the facts and review them with the irate buyer. It is just as true of the large, quantity purchaser as it is of the one-at-a-time customer that an explanation of labor, material, and overhead costs tends to be overlooked. A calm, intelligent explanation or valid justification of the rising costs and how they have affected the selling prices will, more often than not, mollify the situation. Of course, the customer will not say, "Thanks for raising the prices," but he will understand, cool his anger, and, probably, continue to be an active account.

Whether the type of business operation deals in the movement of products or in the delivery of services, it is vital for management to have a pricing policy, establish prices according to costs and market conditions, carry out changes and handle controversy in a way that does not interrupt or damage profitable business. Pricing in any business follows a careful analysis of all cost factors to which is added a reasonable and workable margin. Successful pricing, as viewed by the customer, is a matter of value received for the moneys paid. Effective pricing is one of the keys to business life and growth. Pricing for continued profits is one of the skills that distinguishes the successful business manager.

12

Pricing, Competition, and the Law

PRICING for profit is vital to any business in a free enterprise system. Pricing for survival, or having to price at a loss to meet cutthroat or apparently unfair competition, is as serious as cutting an artery of a living creature; surely it will bleed to death. Yet competition is one of the characteristics of the U.S. business environment. Any firm must compete successfully if it is to stay alive and prosper. But competition does not mean "anything goes." And, fortunately, there are legal safeguards against unfair competition and price discrimination which apply to all companies, regardless of size.

Government regulation of monopolistic and unfair trade practices directly affects and benefits small business. There is a broad body of federal legislation designed to encourage and protect free private enterprise. This legislation includes the Sherman, Clayton, and Federal Trade Commission Acts. The U.S. Department of Justice enforces the federal legislation by prosecuting the violators of such legislation.

Although the Department of Justice is not a service agency furnishing direct aid to small businesses, such firms receive a great measure of indirect assistance from its enforcement of the federal antitrust laws. Small business is generally the primary victim of restraints of trade and of monopolization practices.

The federal antitrust laws were designed to break up or prevent undue concentration of economic power in any business or industry. They prohibit conspiracies to restrain free trade or commerce, monopolization or attempts to monopolize a field, and a variety of practices which may have the effect of substantially lessening or prohibiting competition. The philosophy is that a vigorous prosecution of the antitrust laws maintains a free competition in the American economy, and permits the development and growth of a sound body of small business concerns.

Among the most important agencies providing safeguards for the small business concern is the Federal Trade Commission. Its work is very significant to owners, operators, and managers of small businesses. However, few small businessmen are familiar with the origin and the responsibilities assigned to the FTC by the legislation that created it.

The Federal Trade Commission Act, which created the FTC as an enforcement agency in 1914, prohibits unfair methods of competition and unfair and deceptive acts and practices in commerce.

The Sherman Antitrust Act of 1890 is essentially an antimonopoly law. It was enacted in an era when trusts and combinations exercised power considered dangerous to the public welfare. The fundamental purpose of the Act is to prevent restraints to free competition which tend to limit production, raise prices, or otherwise control a market. It also seeks to secure equal opportunity for businessmen and to protect purchasers of goods and services.

The Clayton Act of 1913 is designed to reach schemes and practices that are discriminating and, under certain circumstances, might lead to the formation of trusts. It supplements the purpose and effect of the Sherman Act. The Clayton Act prohibits price discrimination, knowingly inducing or receiving a discrimination in price, exclusive dealing arrangements and tying contracts, mergers, interlocking directorates, and intercorporate stockholding, all of which may have an adverse effect on competition. Also, it prohibits discrimination in the payments for and the furnishing of services and facilities, and illegal brokerage payments.

Resale Price Maintenance

Resale price maintenance is a system of distribution under which the owner of a trademark or a brand name or, in some cases, any seller of a trademarked or otherwise identified product, establishes the price at which it may be resold. This is done by entering into a contract with at least one distributor and notifying all other distributors in the state, who are then obliged to maintain the price named in the contract.

Agreements fixing resale prices of commodities are invalid under the Sherman and Federal Trade Commission Acts because they have the effect of restraints of trade or unfair methods of competition. In the past, states were able to enact statutes legalizing resale price contracts in *intrastate commerce*. The Miller-Tydings Amendment (1937) to the Sherman Act, and the McGuire Amendment (1952) to the Federal Trade Commission Act permitted exemptions from the federal antitrust laws for agreements making resale prices binding within a state on distributors who do not themselves sign agreements.

Horizontal (group) agreements in which manufacturers, wholesalers, or other resellers fix resale prices violate the provisions of the Sherman Act and the Federal Trade Commission Act. On the other hand, vertical (individual) agreements between a manufacturer and his wholesalers or between a wholesaler and his retailers were legal when permissible in states in which the resale price was established. These were known as "fair trade agreements" and set the minimum retail price at which an item could be sold by every store within those states.

More recently, however, many of the states that permitted manufacturers to establish resale price maintenance were reversing direction: revising, amending, or eliminating such laws. Finally, in December 1975, President Ford signed a bill effectively ending fair trade agreements. The act, which took effect in March 1976, voids the federal law which allowed such agreements in intrastate commerce. This act is intended to "give the consumer a better break in the marketplace" and thus "help restore competition."

Exclusive Deals, Price, and Other Discriminations

Two features of the Clayton Act are especially interesting to and protective of the small businessman. One feature makes it unlawful to create a lease or a sale on condition that the lessee or the purchaser will not use or deal in the products or services of a competitor of the lessor or seller, where the effect might be substantially to lessen competition. The other feature prohibits price discrimination where the effect is to lessen competition.

The famous *Robinson-Patman Act* of 1936 amended the provisions of the Clayton Act which deal with price discrimination. Generally, with certain exceptions, it prohibits any direct or indirect discrimination in price between different purchasers of commodities of like grade and quality where the effect might be substantially to lessen competition.

Prices may be varied in accordance with differences in cost, which must be justified by the seller. In addition, price differentials are permitted as the result of changes in the value of the product or in market conditions, and where commodities are not of like grade or quality.

You May Choose Your Customers

The Clayton Act as amended by the Robinson-Patman Act provides that sellers shall not be prevented from selecting their own customers in bona fide transactions which are not in restraint of trade. While price discriminations are prohibited, the right of individual traders to discriminate in the choice of customers was reaffirmed. Further, not only are price discriminations by sellers prohibited, but buyers who knowingly induce or receive illegal price discriminations are guilty of violation. This provision is of special interest and importance to the small businessman who is caught in the negotiating vise of a big-business customer or supplier.

There are additional provisions of the Clayton Act which prohibit discriminatory allowances or payments to favored customers for services or facilities furnished by them, or the discriminatory furnishing of services or facilities to favored customers by the seller in connection with the distribution of his product.

Anticompetitive Mergers

The Clayton Act originally prohibited intercorporate stock acquisitions in instances where the effect may be a substantial curtailment of competition in any section or community. However, this did not stop corporations from acquiring the assets of other corporations. This impaired the effectiveness of the Clayton Act.

The Celler Amendment (1950) corrected this situation by prohibiting the acquisition of the whole or any part of the assets of another corporation when the acquisition may effect a substantial curtailment of competition or tend to create a monopoly. The Amendment relates to commerce in any section of the country rather than in any section of a community. Therefore, the stock or asset merger of two small companies which would eliminate competition between them would be prohibited if other competitors in that line of commerce were so few or relatively small that the merger would produce a significant change in the intensity of competition in any section of the country.

The courts have held that this provision of the Celler Amendment does not apply to the sale of stock or assets to a competitor by a company in a failing or bankrupt condition.

Unfair Business Practices

Government regulation of improper business practices was expanded by the Federal Trade Commission Act, which prohibited "unfair methods of competition in commerce." Determination of what constituted an unfair method of competition was left to the Federal Trade Commission and the courts.

The powers of the Commission were extended under the *Wheeler-Lea Act* (1938) which also declared unlawful "unfair or deceptive acts or practices in commerce" whether or not in competition. In addition, the Act expressly provides that the dissemination of any false advertising through the Unites States mails, or in commerce by any means, for the purpose of inducing the purchase of certain commodities constitutes an unfair or deceptive practice.

FTC activities include legal activities to enforce the prohibition against unfair methods of competition and unfair or deceptive practices. Some typical methods and practices that have been condemned in the Commission's cease and desist orders include making false and disparaging statements regarding competitors' products and businesses, selling rebuilt, second-hand, and old articles as new, passing off goods as products of competitors by simulating trade names or labels, bribing customers' employees to obtain patronage, buying up supplies for the purpose of hampering competitors, and stifling or eliminating competition.

Enforcement of Laws

With a few exceptions, enforcement and administration of the federal antitrust and related laws are centered in the

Federal Trade Commission and the Department of Justice. Complaints by small businessmen about suspected violations by competitors usually form the basis for a large part of the antitrust investigations. Under the Sherman and Clayton Acts a small business injured by an antitrust violation may itself bring suit in the federal courts and recover several times the provable damages.

Examples of Illegal Practices

Price fixing. A pricing agreement among competitors is illegal under the Sherman Act and the Federal Trade Commission Act. The United States Supreme Court has ruled that under the Sherman Act a combination formed for the purpose and with the effect of raising, depressing, fixing, pegging, or stabilizing the price of a commodity in interstate or foreign commerce is illegal per se.

Exclusive deals. The Clayton Act declares it illegal for a seller to make sales conditional upon a buyer's promise not to make purchases from the seller's competition, if this type of sale may result in substantial lessening of competition. The law also prohibits a seller from making a buyer promise that he will purchase all his requirements of similar commodities from the seller when this has the same effect on competition.

False and deceptive advertising. A wide range of court decisions have emphasized the fact that a seller violates the Federal Trade Commission Act if he misrepresents his product in a material respect, or if he fails to disclose pertinent information, where such practice has the tendency or capacity to mislead and deceive purchasers or prospective purchasers, or to injure competition.

Price discrimination. The Clayton Act as amended by the Robinson-Patman Act prohibits price discrimination which may result in a substantial lessening of or injury to competition. This means not only injury to competitors of a seller, but also injury to purchasers who are damaged because their competitors receive unjustifiably low prices or unjustifiable discounts.

Payment of brokerage to buyers. The Robinson-Patman Act forbids a seller to pay brokerage to a buyer. This is true whether payments are made directly or through third parties who eventually hand over the money to the purchaser.

Guides to the Truth

One of the founders of the Federal Trade Commission stated that honest businessmen want something more than the negative possibility of legal process to back them up. In his opinion, they want the positive advice and guidance that an interstate trade body can give them. As a result, the FTC has published several guides that deal specifically with fictitious pricing. The issues are:

Savings claims. Sellers must not imply that they are offering a lower price than other merchants unless that price applies to a specific article, not just similar or comparable merchandise. Furthermore, any savings claims must be based on a reduction from the usual retail price of the article in the trading area where the statement is made, that is, from the advertiser's regular price.

Pricing problem. Merchandise must not be advertised as reduced in price if the former higher price is based on an artificial markup or on previous infrequent sales. The "former higher price" quoted must also be the one that immediately preceded the new bargain price in the recent regular course of business; if it is not, this fact must be clearly disclosed.

Comparable merchandise. Comparative prices for comparable merchandise may be used only if the claim makes it clear that the advertiser is talking only about comparable merchandise and not the former or regular price of the article he is selling. Also, the comparable merchandise must be obtainable at the comparative price in the same trade area (or, if not, the ad must clearly say so).

Special sales prices. Such prices must not be advertised

unless they represent a bona fide reduction from the seller's customary retail price of a saving from the regular price in that trade area.

Two-for-one sales. No such claims may be made unless the sale price of the two articles is the seller's usual retail price for the single article in the recent regular course of his business, or is the usual price in the trade area.

Special sales claims. So-called half-price or 50-percent-off or one-cent sales must be factually true, and, if conditioned upon the purchase of additional merchandise, this fact must be conspicuously disclosed. Moreover, the proffered price reduction must be from the advertiser's customary and recent price.

"Factory" and "wholesale" ads. Products must not be advertised to the consuming public at "factory" or "wholesale" prices unless they are actually being offered at the same prices retailers regularly pay to their suppliers.

Fictitious preticketing. No article should be preticketed with any price figure that exceeds the price at which the article is usually sold in the trade area where the product is being offered for sale. Those who furnish the fictitiously high price tags are equally culpable with the merchants who use them. The same prohibition applies to material such as display placards on which are printed a fictitiously high price for the product offered for sale.

Comparative prices. These are taboo in the sale of articles described as "imperfect," "irregulars," or "seconds" unless the higher comparative price actually was, and is conspicuously shown to be, for the same article in new and perfect condition. Also, the comparative price should not be used unless it is the same at which the advertiser usually sells the product without defects or is the regular price in the trading area for the merchandise when perfect.

Jurisdiction

Generally speaking, the Federal Trade Commission, before it can assert jurisdiction, must make a showing that the misrepresented product has been shipped by the seller to a consumer in another state, or that the proposed respondent is part of an interstate operation.

Deceptive price representations, which are local in nature, are subject to the provisions of the statutes of the state in which the acts take place.

Specific Antitrust Practices

The Antitrust Division of the Department of Justice has always been eager to assist the small business firm in problems involving violations of the federal antitrust laws. The great majority of antitrust investigations and cases are initiated as a result of complaints from the public. It is often difficult to determine what constitutes violations of the antitrust laws. Nevertheless, the small-business manager should be aware of some of the business practices in which the Department of Justice is especially interested:

□ Any agreement to fix or regulate prices.

□ Any boycotting activities involving, for example, members of a trade association agreeing to exclude competitors or a businessman inducing suppliers to withhold supplies from a competitor.

□ Tie-in sales in which a businessman will sell a product, either patented or unpatented, to a customer only if the latter will purchase another product as well.

□ Full-line forcing of products, whereby the purchaser must take all of his supplier's line of products or get none at all.

□ Agreements by competitors to assign each other separate sales territories and to refrain from competing in each other's territories.

□ Discriminatory pricing for some customers at the expense of others by means of rebates, discounts, service charges, and other excuses for price differentials.

□ The obtaining, by a business or group of businesses in an industry, of a percentage of the market sufficient to give it the power to control prices and exclude competition.

▫ The merger of two corporations, by a transfer of stock or of assets, which may substantially lessen competition or tend to create a monopoly.

▫ Various general predatory practices, such as business espionage or the policing of competitors to ensure that they conform to the industry's traditions and customs.

If, as a small-business owner or manager you have observed any of these practices in your business experience or if your business has suffered as a result of such practices by competitors or suppliers, you can bring the facts to the attention of the Department of Justice, either in Washington, D.C., or at one of the several field offices located in major cities across the country.

It must be understood that, to enable the Department to make an accurate analysis of the problem, it is essential that all the facts be provided in as much detail as possible. Include a description of the business or industry involved, all relevant dates, names and addresses of the parties, an indication of the size, importance, and percentage of the market held by each business involved. If you provide the Department with copies of relevant documents such as ads, price sheets, agreements, letters, memos, or minutes of meetings, it will more readily comprehend the significance of the alleged violation and much time will be saved. In time, an agent of the Antitrust Division or of the Federal Bureau of Investigation may be assigned to make direct contact with you as part of the process of determining whether or not any federal laws have in fact been violated.

Although the large company is more vulnerable and has more exposure to the possibility of violating federal laws by virtue of the fact that it engages regularly in interstate commerce, the small business is liable for any similar illegal actions. Perhaps, in view of all that has been pointed out about the widely ranging federal laws of commerce and the agencies that enforce these laws, it becomes obvious why big business corporations maintain their own legal departments in addition to using outside firms as legal specialists.

It is not unusual for a big business to maintain on its staff a lawyer who specializes, for example, in the effects of the Robinson-Patman Act and fulfills regularly the function of counseling the marketing department of his corporation.

The successful small-business manager may not be able to afford the service of a full-time staff lawyer; however, he should have a sensitivity to the restraints of the law which are designed to protect him as well as his competitors.

13

How to Read
Financial Statements

THE size of a company is often measured in terms of its assets or sales. In both cases the significance of the figure is entirely relative. It must be judged against the background of the industry. For example, the assets of a railroad may numerically exceed those of a department store, yet the railroad may be considered small in its field and the store considered large.

How can you get to see the dollar figures for the assets or sales of a company? Wouldn't it be nice to know exactly how big or small each of your competitors is? If your competitor is publicly held, that is to say, if ownership in the company has been offered to the public through the issuance of stock, it is mandatory that the company regularly publish financial statements, which then become public knowledge.

"Financial statements? Isn't that technical stuff? Not in my line! Ask my accountant." Yes, financial statements are technical. But if you are to be a successful business manager, you must make it part of your "line" to understand and interpret the data they offer. Sure, your accountant can probably read and understand them, even put one together for your company. However, if you can't interpret it, how are you going to make important decisions related to managing, to spending, or to borrowing money? Ask your accountant? If he's smart, and he probably is, he will help you with the interpretation and offer advice when asked, but he will not make your decisions for you—even though the subject is purely related to finances. He's not the business manager. You are. If your background is that of a certified public accountant with field experience, you are way out ahead. Move past "Go" and collect your reward. However, if, as is more likely, you are among those who do not have an accountant's technical skills, read on—this chapter is directed especially to you!

The time will come, more than once, when you are eyeball to eyeball with creditors, stockholders, partners, bankers, or potential moneylenders and they will ask some incisive questions about your business finances. If you are trying to gain an infusion of cash from a bank, the loan officer will in part measure you on the basis of your statistical record and your financial sophistication.

Assume you are the manager or owner of a privately held company. You may own it all yourself, or you and your family or friends are the sole investors, or you manage it for a private group. Financial information or statements of the financial condition of the company do not have to be made available for public view. Certainly, you and your partners or investors must know periodically how well (or poorly) the company is doing so that management decisions can be made.

When one talks about how well a company is doing, it all boils down to dollars and cents. If this information and its interpretation are left entirely to the accountant, the businessman in effect abdicates part of the control of his business. This may explain why some businesses never get too far off the ground, why some businesses are plagued by crisis after crisis, why some businesses do not succeed. Without financial control, a business becomes lopsided. It runs away from its manager, eventually crashes or fizzles out of existence.

Financial statements of the condition of a business are essentially contained in two important documents. One is the *balance sheet*. The other is the *profit-and-loss* or *earnings statement,* colloquially referred to as the *P&L* (or the *income) statement.* The difference between the two is often explained by comparing the balance sheet to a still picture and the P&L to a moving picture. The balance sheet presents a financial picture of the business as it was on a specific date, usually the last day of a calendar month. It answers the question, How did the business stand financially *on that date?* The P&L measures expenses against sales revenues over a definite period of time, such as a month or a year, to show the net profit or loss derived from operations *for the entire period.*

The Balance Sheet

A balance sheet is always dated specifically for one day. It has two sections. The first section shows the *assets.* The second section shows the *liabilities* (debts) and the *owner's equity* (investment), which together represent the claims against the assets. The assets may be listed above the liabilities, or the two may be grouped side by side, with the assets shown to the left of the liabilities. The total assets always equal the total liabilities: One balances the other, hence the name "balance sheet." Figure 7 is a balance sheet for a fictional but typical retailer.

This balance sheet for the PQD Store presents the financial position on June 30, 19__. The total of the assets is offset by liabilities and equity. The balance sheet balances. Depreciation and other factors reduce the value of some assets. It is important to state the value correctly in the balance sheet. Therefore, the balance sheet is set up in a way that demonstrates that provision has been made for reductions in value by using depreciation, or valuation, accounts. Some of

Figure 7. Balance sheet for a typical retailer.

THE PQD STORE
Balance Sheet
June 30, 19___

ASSETS

Current assets			
Cash		$20,000	
Accounts receivable	$40,000		
Less allowance for doubtful accounts	3,000	37,000	
Inventories	$45,000		
Less allowance for inventory loss	5,000	40,000	
Total current assets			$97,000
Fixed assets			
Machinery	$20,000		
Less allowance for depreciation	4,000	$16,000	
Buildings	28,000		
Less allowance for depreciation	6,000	22,000	
Land		12,000	
Total fixed assets			50,000
Total assets			$147,000

LIABILITIES AND EQUITY

Current liabilities		
Accounts payable	$20,000	
Notes payable	30,000	
Accrued liabilities	6,000	
Allowance for taxes	4,000	
Total current liabilities		$60,000
Equity		
Capital stock	$50,000	
Surplus	37,000	
Total equity		87,000
Total liabilities and equity		$147,000

the more common of these accounts include accounts receivable, losses in the value of inventories, and fixed assets.

Accounts receivable are analyzed according to the length of time the money has been considered to be receivable. An estimate is made of the amount that is forecast to be uncollectible. This is an allowance for probable bad debts and is usually computed for a given accounting period, treated either as a percentage of the average balance of receivables or as a percentage of the net credit sales for the period. It is shown on the balance sheet as a deduction from "accounts receivable" under "assets."

Losses in the value of inventories may occur as a result of price changes, physical deterioration, style changes or other obsoleting factors, pilferage, and so on. If such losses are likely to occur, an estimate of possible shrinkage should be made. Past history or experience is the only tool available for such a forecast. This estimate appears on the balance sheet as a deduction from "inventories" under "assets."

Fixed assets other than land decline in value as they are used. The decline may be caused by wear and tear, technical obsolescence, or any other factors that make them less valuable than when acquired. A periodic charge for depreciation should be made and shown on the balance sheet as a deduction from the value of the assets.

Figure 8 is the balance sheet for a fictional but typical medium-size manufacturing business, QRO Manufacturing Company. Note that "inventories" under "current assets" are detailed as "finished products," "work in process," "raw materials," and "supplies." Finished products are merchandise completed and ready for sale. Work in process consists of goods in the process of manufacture but not yet completed. Raw materials consist of materials to be used in production. Supplies are materials that are used in connection with the processing but that do not of themselves become products. Because this business is more complex than that represented in Figure 7, the balance sheet is much more detailed.

Figure 8. Balance sheet for a typical manufacturer.

QRO MANUFACTURING COMPANY
Balance Sheet
July 31, 19__

ASSETS

Current assets			
Cash		$40,000	
Accounts receivable	$90,000		
Less allowance for doubtful accounts	10,000	80,000	
Inventories			
Finished products	75,000		
Work in process	75,000		
Raw materials	20,000		
Supplies	10,000	180,000	
Prepaid expenses		10,000	
Total current assets			$310,000
Fixed assets			
Furniture and fixtures	10,000		
Less allowance for depreciation	5,000	5,000	
Machinery and equipment	30,000		
Less allowance for depreciation	16,000	14,000	
Buildings	45,000		
Less allowance for depreciation	9,000	36,000	
Land		15,000	
Total fixed assets			70,000
Investments			20,000
Total assets			$400,000

Figure 8. (continued)

LIABILITIES AND EQUITY

Current liabilities			
Accounts payable		$40,000	
Notes payable		80,000	
Accrued liabilities			
Wages & salaries payable	$4,000		
Interest payable	1,000	5,000	
Allowance for taxes			
Income tax	$16,000		
State taxes	4,000	20,000	
Total current liabilities			$145,000
Equity			
Capital stock		$200,000	
Surplus		55,000	
Total equity			255,000
Total liabilities and equity			$400,000

The Profit-and-Loss Statement

This is the payoff document for many potential investors and creditors. It shows how much the company makes or loses during the entire year of operations. While the balance sheet shows the fundamental soundness of a company by reflecting its financial position at a given date, the P&L statement is usually of greater interest to investors and lenders because it shows the record of operating activities over a longer period of time. A historical record of P&L data serves as a valuable guide in anticipating how the company may do in the future.

This P&L statement matches the amounts received from selling the goods and other items of income against all the costs and outlays incurred in order to operate the company. The result is a *net profit* (or a *net loss*) for the year. The costs incurred are usually the cost of the goods sold, depreciation, interest on money borrowed, taxes and overhead expenses such as wages and salaries, rent, utilities, and supplies. Unlike the balance sheet, there is no balancing or equalizing of assets and liabilities in the P&L statement. The bottom line of the statement is net profit for the year.

Figure 9 is the P&L statement for the same retailer whose balance sheet was displayed in Figure 7.

The small manufacturer converts raw materials into finished goods; therefore, his method of accounting for cost of goods sold differs from the method for retailers or wholesalers. Computing the cost of goods sold during the accounting period involves beginning and ending inventories, as with the retailer and wholesaler. But in manufacturing it involves not only the finished goods inventories, but also inventories of raw materials, work in process, direct labor, and factory-overhead costs.

In order to avoid a long and complicated P&L, the cost of goods manufactured is usually reported as a separate statement. Figures 10 and 11 show how both statements might be done by a typical small manufacturer, the fictitious ACW Company.

Figure 9.   P&L statement for a typical retailer.

THE PQD STORE

Profit-and-Loss Statement
For the Year Ended December 31, 19__

Sales		$360,000
Cost of goods sold		210,000
Gross margin		$150,000
Selling expenses		
Salaries	$45,000	
Commission	15,000	
Advertising	15,000	
Total selling expenses		75,000
Selling margin		$75,000
Administrative expenses		30,000
Net profit		$45,000

Figure 10. ACW Company's statement of cost of goods manufactured.

ACW COMPANY

Statement of Cost of Goods Manufactured
For the Year Ended December 31, 19__

Work-in-process inventory, January 1, 19__			$18,800
Raw materials			
Inventory, January 1, 19__		$154,300	
Purchases		263,520	
Freight-in		9,400	
Cost of materials available for use		$427,220	
Less inventory, December 31, 19__		163,120	
Cost of materials used		264,100	
Direct labor		150,650	
Manufacturing overhead			
Indirect labor	$23,750		
Factory heat, light, and power	89,500		
Factory supplies used	22,100		
Insurance and taxes	8,100		
Depreciation of plant and equipment	35,300		
Total manufacturing overhead		178,750	
Total manufacturing costs			593,500
Total work in process during period			612,300
Less work-in-process inventory, Dec. 31, 19__			42,600
Cost of goods manufactured			$569,700

Figure 11. ACW Company's P&L statement.

Profit-and-Loss Statement
For the Year Ended December 31, 19__

Net sales			$669,100
Cost of goods sold			
Finished goods inventory, January 1, 19__		$ 69,200	
Cost of goods manufactured (Figure 10)		569,700	
Total cost of goods available for sale		638,900	
Less finished goods inventory, December 31, 19__		66,400	
Cost of goods sold			572,500
Gross margin			96,600
Selling and administrative expenses			
Selling expenses			
Sales salaries and commissions	$26,700		
Advertising expense	12,900		
Miscellaneous selling expense	2,100		
Total selling expenses		$41,700	
Administrative expenses			
Salaries	27,400		
Miscellaneous administrative expenses	4,800		
Total administrative expenses		32,200	
Total selling & administrative expenses			73,900
Net operating profit			$22,700
Other revenue			15,300
Net profit before taxes			$38,000
Estimated income tax			12,640
Net profit after income tax			$25,360

Be Aware of the Limitations

The balance sheet and the P&L statement, one must remember, are both reports of historical activity. They do not, per se, tell the reader exactly what is going to happen in the future. However, because something more substantial is lacking and some basis for estimating probable future movement is required, these two documents are generally accepted as primary source data. Although the details of the content, form, and arrangement of general-purpose financial statements may vary to suit the circumstances, such statements should meet reporting standards that assure adequate disclosure.

Financial statements should be audited by independent auditors to provide assurance to the reader that they represent the financial results of the business fairly and in accordance with generally accepted accounting methods, applied consistently. More often than not, an unaudited financial statement will be unacceptable to a bank or other lending institution, or to the financial managers of a major supplier from whom the business manager may be seeking a substantial line of credit.

Exercise Critical Analysis

There often are differences of opinion in appraising many of the items displayed in a P&L statement or in a balance sheet. Even the most detailed, the most elaborate multicolored statement must be subjected to careful scrutiny. (The point here is that your own statements will similarly be carefully scrutinized.) It is important to examine some of the principal items and the practices that may tend to distort the real situation. Whether or not this distortion is introduced deliberately or through naivety is not important; the effect is important.

Reported earnings can be distorted by (1) an overstatement or understatement of major items of expense or of income, (2) subjective estimates for depreciation, and (3) treatment of nonrecurring and nonoperating gains and losses. It is important to know whether the P&L statement is prepared on a cash or an accrual basis.

The *cash basis* reflects only income and expenditures resulting from actual cash receipts and cash disbursements. Most business is conducted on credit, and these transactions are not shown in a way that adequately reflects their effects on gains and losses for the period.

The *accrual basis* takes into account all transactions, whether cash or credit is used. However, one must be aware of the fact that a sale made in the middle of the month is reported on the balance sheet as part of gross revenue for that month, although payment will be received in a later month. On the cash basis the amount of the sale is excluded from the balance sheet for the month in which the sale has been made and appears in the report for the month in which payment is actually received. Unless it is specifically stated to be otherwise, a P&L statement is presumed to have been prepared on the accrual basis.

Expenses are affected by judgments of the management. Charges made against income are in some cases determined by management rather than by actual obligations incurred or by cash expended. Examples of this are provisions for depreciation, amortization, doubtful accounts, allowances for inventory loss, and reserves for contingencies. Other expenses subject to the discretion of management are maintenance and repairs, rents, contract labor, bonuses to officers and directors, and reserves for estimated taxes.

Thus, one can see that it is essential to understand the practices and principles observed by the management of the company in preparing the financial statements. It is possible to control or even manipulate (with all that word implies) expenses and the resultant net profit data to show a lesser or greater amount. The sophisticated "analyst" seeks disclosure in the financial statements of pertinent facts related to these items, together with an explanation of the policy followed. Only then is he in a position to develop a meaningful interpretation of the documents.

Who Uses Financial Statements?

There are at least three groups who are interested in the financial data of a business enterprise: owners or investors, management, and creditors. The first are primarily interested in a basis for estimating the company's earning power. Management is primarily interested in a tool that will measure costs and efficiency to facilitate intelligent decisions. Credit men and commercial banks are concerned primarily with liquidity and ability to pay debts and short-term obligations. The same financial statements are used by all three groups for their own purposes.

If you have been to the bank for a business loan of substantial size, it is probable you were asked to provide P&L statements for the past three to five years, assuming you have been in operation for at least that long. The loan officer or the lender was doing an *analysis by comparison,* comparing reports of current status with those of related previous accounting periods in an effort to determine trends in sales, expenses, and profits. These trends are more than mere numbers; they provide the lender or creditor with a factor of confidence in you as a manager of a business enterprise in which he is being asked to make an investment.

He, too, is motivated to be successful.

14

What's Your
Return on Investment?

WHERE do you keep your money? In a bank? In a savings and loan association account? Do you own stocks or bonds? Do you receive dividends or interest payments? Do you hold an interest-paying mortgage on a piece of land or a building? Do you have equity in some company? If any of the above applies to you, you are an investor and you probably have a good hard number which tells you your annual *return on investment*, that is, how much each of the investments returns to you on an annual basis.

If you own 1,000 shares of common stock for which you paid $10,000 and you receive a quarterly dividend check for $250 (25¢ dividend per share per quarter), or $1,000 for a full year, your annual return on this investment is 10 percent ($1,000 ÷ $10,000). If your bank savings account stands at $13,246, for example, and it pays 5 percent interest per annum, your annual return on this investment is 5 percent. In common stock ownership there is no guarantee of dividends. However, the bank guarantees the dividend payment (interest rate) and for this guarantee, or assurance of security for your investment, provides a lower rate of return on investment.

Suppose, further, that you also have invested $9,500 in one company for 25 percent ownership. The $9,500 may or may not have been all in cash; some of it may have been in materials or equipment. No matter at this point. That company reports an after-tax profit of $3,420, which is then paid out to the owners as a dividend or bonus. Your share of the net profits is $855. This means you have a return of 9 percent on your original investment ($855 ÷ $9,500).

Imagine, too, that you had taken advantage of another apparent opportunity and had invested $1,200 in a friend's business venture. At the end of his first year of operation, he paid you a share of the profits in the form of $125 cash. Your annual return on the investment was 10.4 percent. Which of the two investments was more profitable, the $9,500 or the $1,200? In terms of percentages, quite clearly the $1,200 investment was the better of the two, even though the $9,500 investment returned a greater number of dollars. In fact, it is a better (by .4 percent) investment than the $10,000 purchase of 1,000 shares of common stock.

Many more examples could be presented. However, they would quickly become repetitious of the principle that return on investment, colloquially referred to as ROI, is an important, very significant measure of the merit of success of a business venture. It does not provide a measure of the safety or security of the investment, only of its performance during an accounting period, expressed as a percentage.

Of all the measures of business success that are in use today, it is probable that the most popular and meaningful one for the small businessman is return on investment. Accountants, financial analysts, bankers, investors, lenders, and business managers of profit centers use ROI as basic data for judging the health of a specific company or division. Companies and divisions, large or small, are expanded, closed, born, bought, or sold on the basis of ROI data. No company is too large or too small for ROI analysis. So, it is appropriate to be familiar with the fundamentals of ROI and to apply them as one measure of the condition of your company or any segment of it which is measured on a P&L basis.

Putting Financial Data to Work

In preceding chapters we discussed record keeping which leads to accurate financial statements. Now we are truly beginning to make use of the data so painstakingly accumulated as we enter the decision-making aspects of business management. The simplest way to determine ROI is to divide the net profit on sales by the total investment. The basic formula then looks like this:

$$18.4\% \text{ (ROI)} = \frac{\$23,254 \text{ (net profit)}}{\$126,500 \text{ (total investment)}}$$

A 20 percent reduction in investment with the same profit of $23,254 would increase the ROI by 20 percent. One could conclude that, ideally, no dollar investment at all should be made in the business. This conclusion would be just as unrealistic as the contention that there should be no expenses of any kind in the operation of a business, that it should all be profit.

The real world requires that an investment be made in some form, using either a negotiable commodity such as money or a measurable asset in the form of equipment, such as an automobile. Realistically, time can be equated with money. The one-man company which doesn't pay its "staff" any salary or does not measure costs of getting around town in the owner's personal car on company business is simply not keeping records of its true investments, costs, and obligations. An investment is being made in the company's operations; it is just not being recorded.

Even if the one-man company is a manufacturer's rep working on straight commission and without an inventory requirement, it would be erroneous to conclude that the first commission check received is all profit. An investment has been made in time, travel, and out-of-pocket expenses. A return on the investment has been made. Good or bad, a return on investment can be calculated as a measure of commercial effectiveness. An accurate conclusion would be to keep investment as low as possible and profits as high as possible.

Comparisons Are Meaningful

All analyses of accounting data involve comparisons. A statement that the ABC Company earned $750,000 in profits is not useful unless it is compared with something else. The comparison may be intuitive or it may be statistical. If the ABC Company is an industrial giant with thousands of people on the payroll, intuition tells us that $750,000 in profit is not very good. We have developed the impression that a company the size of ABC should earn much more money. A statistical comparison might be formalized by comparing ABC's earnings of $750,000 with the profits of past years, or by comparing it with averages for the industry. Whatever the standard of comparison, it is the comparison that makes the statement of profit meaningful.

Inasmuch as ROI can be measured quantitatively, the overall objective of a business is to earn a satisfactory return on the investment in it, consistent with maintaining a sound financial position. The ROI is calculated from and relates to the main categories appearing on the balance sheet and P&L statement. A portion of the current assets is offset by current liabilities, and investors must furnish only the remainder, which is called working capital. They must also furnish the funds for noncurrent assets.

The return on investment measurement recognizes the value of capital, that owners could use their funds to advantage in other ventures, and that capital is seldom available in unlimited quantities. ROI emphasizes the importance of the economical use of capital in the operation of the firm. Use of ROI as a measure of performance provides management with a broad avenue for performance improvement. ROI can be understood throughout an organization and can be applied equally to all groups, subsidiaries, and divisions of a corporation.

In using an ROI formula, it is absolutely essential that consistency be employed in the definitions of terms. For example, it does not matter whether "profit" be construed as "before" or as "after" taxes, or whether "total assets" or "owners' equity" be used to describe "investment," as long as the definition chosen is adhered to consistently.

Return on investment can be usefully calculated both in terms of the return on the *asset investment* and also on that portion of the investment funds of the business that is supplied by the owners. The ROI can be simply calculated as follows in a direct formula:

$$\text{ROI} = \frac{\text{net profit after taxes}}{\text{total assets}}$$

A less direct method of calculating ROI, known as the "turnover method," is more revealing:

$$\text{ROI} = \frac{\text{sales}}{\text{assets}} \times \frac{\text{net profit}}{\text{sales}}$$

By way of illustration, the XYZ Company has total assets of $200,000, annual sales of $500,000, and net income after taxes of $20,000. The direct formula ($20,000 ÷ $200,000) shows the ROI to be 10 percent.

Using the turnover method, we find the following:

$$\text{ROI} = \frac{\$500,000}{\$200,000} \times \frac{\$20,000}{\$500,000}$$

$$= 2.5 \times 4\%$$

$$= 10\%$$

Since the results of the two formulas are the same, why use the longer turnover method? Let's try an example of changes in some of the factors and see how the turnover formula reveals the specific effects.

Assume that the XYZ Company increases its sales in the next year to $600,000 and net income after taxes to $24,000, a linear increment of 20 percent. However, suppose that in order to achieve this growth in sales and profits, total assets had to be increased to $300,000; this is not an unlikely situation. The direct formula quickly tells us that the ROI dropped to 8 percent. Calculating by the turnover method reveals an important fact:

$$\text{ROI} = \frac{\$600,000}{\$300,000} \times \frac{\$24,000}{\$600,000}$$

$$= 2 \times 4\%$$

$$= 8\%$$

The fact highlighted is that the profit on sales held constant at 4 percent and that is was the large increase in asset investment related to sales that was responsible for the lower ROI. Use of the turnover formula reveals that, in order to maintain the same ROI of 10 percent, the asset investment should have been controlled to restrict the maximum increase to $240,000 ($600,000 ÷ $240,000 = 2.5). It becomes apparent that increases in sales or profit returns on sales enhance return on investment only if the total of assets is held to a less than proportional increase. Thus we see a method for making management decisions and establishing continuing controls.

There are numerous other methods, using financial or accounting information, for measuring and comparing the performance of a company over a finite accounting period of operations. Some of these will be explored in the next chapters.

15

How to Use Ratios to Measure Your Success

"HOW'S it going, Joe?"

"Great, Mac! The bottom line of my financial statement says I made a nice profit."

"Good. But that tells you part of the story of where you've been. How are you going to figure out where to go? Joe, there's a lot of information contained in your balance sheet and in your year-end financial statement that can be put to excellent use in analyzing your business and, more important, helping you make intelligent management decisions."

"I've heard that before, Mac. But isn't that just some more of the technical stuff that my accountant gets paid for?"

"Joe, your accountant is paid to accumulate and display the data. You, not he, are the manager of the business. The final decisions are still up to you and your active investors. Sure, your accountant is vital to doing some of the complex arithmetic. But there's a good part of management arithmetic you can do yourself so that you don't have to bug your accountant every time you have a new number."

"Sometimes, I must admit, my accountant is not immediately available, even if I could afford to pay him for all the time and advice he can give. But sometimes I look at all the numbers he hands me, and I don't understand them. I know they're significant and important to me, but I'm too embarrassed to admit my lack of deep knowledge of financial analysis. I don't want him to think I'm a dummy, incapable of doing my job."

"Joe, you've just pointed out several very important things. One, you recognize the importance of the accountant's role in your business. Two, you know that time plays an important part in management decisions, and these decisions have to have some basis in numerical facts. Also, even though you're doing an adequate job as a business manager, you want to do still better. Very positive views. However, your accountant won't consider you to be a dummy each time you admit you don't really understand the numbers bit. That's an ego thing only you can control.

"Most important of all, you don't have to have an advanced degree in mathematics to analyze and put to work much of the information contained in the balance sheet and the financial statement. That applies whether you're reading your own or somebody else's numbers. Have you ever heard of *ratio analysis?*"

Analysis of Past Performance

An analytical review of past performance of a company is vital to all groups concerned with the welfare of an enterprise. Management is responsible for the care and preservation of the owners' or stockholders' investments in accordance with the objectives of the business. One of the many measures of the success of management is its ability to anticipate negative situations and put into effect policies and practices that will counter, or at least minimize, the impact of the negative potential. Management has to care for and preserve the owners' and stockholders' investments but, equally important, it must use these investments in a way that produces growth.

The management of any company is usually responsible for the forward movement of the company. Management develops programs, policies, and practices that give maximum assurance that such forward movement will take place. Management continually reviews the past to discover weaknesses as a guide to what may be expected in the future, if present policies and practices are continued. Top management studies any proposed changes in detail and makes every effort to evaluate the alternatives available and the impact each might have on the company's progress if it were implemented. At some point in the considerations, a decision is reached, plans are made or revised, and programs are implemented and monitored.

In making judgments of the effectiveness of decisions and actions, factors of care and preservation of capital (owners' and stockholders' investments), profitability, and progressiveness may be grouped to show the following: (1) adequacy and use of working capital, (2) status and productivity of the plant and equipment, (3) composition of assets and equities, (4) movement of assets and equities, (5) efficiency of operations, and (6) position of capital stock (if such is outstanding) and corporate debt.

What Are Ratios?

A ratio is simply one number expressed in terms of another. Dividing one number, the base, into another is the method. A percentage is one kind of ratio. The base is taken to be 100, and the quotient is expressed as "per hundred" in terms of the base.

Balance sheets and financial statements are chock-full of numbers. Numerous ratios could be computed from a single set of sheets and statements. One could easily become lost in a veritable morass of information, confounded and confused as to just what to do with all this seemingly significant data. However, only a few of the ratios may be helpful in any given situation.

We will describe some of the ratios most frequently used in financial analysis and management decision making. The best approach is not to compute all of them routinely but rather to decide which ratios might be relevant to the specific investigation being made and then to compute only these ratios.

Fundamentally, financial ratios can be grouped into three categories: tests of profitability, tests of liquidity, and tests of solvency. Of course, there is a fourth category which may be called "overall ratios," which are often used in studies comparing companies within the same industry or in comparisons of several accounting periods for the same company.

Tests of Profitability

The *gross profit percentage* as reported in the financial statement indicates the average margin obtained on all products sold. Because it is an average, it does not necessarily represent the margin on individual products. These margins may vary widely from product to product, some being over, others under the average profit productivity. The *net income percentage* is a measure of overall profitability. Many managements consider it to be the most important single measure of a company's performance (or of the management's skills). This may not be the best way to measure performance or skills because the net profit percentage does not reflect the amount of investment needed to earn the income, as the following example illustrates.

Consider two retail operations. Company A operates a supermarket. Company B operates a department store. Operating results of each are summarized and compared.

	A	B
Sales	$10,000,000	$10,000,000
Profit	100,000	1,000,000
Total investment	1,000,000	5,000,000
Return on sales	1%	10%
Return on investment	10%	20%

Supermarkets typically operate on a low gross margin, which is reflected in the small return on sales (1%) compared with the larger return (10%) for the department store, Company B. However, note that the return on investment for Company B is only twice that of Company A, despite the fact that B's profits were ten times greater than A's.

Tests of Liquidity

Liquidity is a company's ability to meet its current obligations. *Liquidity ratios* have to do with current assets, from which current liabilities or obligations will be met. A company that has adequate liquidity may be considered to be in a sound financial position. The current assets divided by the current liabilities are the *current ratio*. This is the most commonly used of all balance sheet ratios. It is not only a measure of the company's liquidity, it is a measure of the margin of safety allowed by management for the unevenness in the flow of funds through the current assets and current liabilities accounts. A company can rarely count on the smooth flow of funds. It needs a supply of ready funds to be assured of being able to pay its bills when they come due. The current ratio indicates the size of this cushion.

Although "snapshot," static figures may be used in making business judgments, business itself is dynamic. Current assets will not be used to liquidate, or reduce to zero, the current liabilities in an operating business firm because as some liabilities are paid off others are being created.

When interpreting the current ratio, consider the proportion of various types of assets. A company with a high percentage of its current assets in cash is more liquid than one with a high percentage in inventory, even though the companies mathematically produce the same current ratio.

The *acid-test ratio* (also called the *quick ratio*) is often used to test the current viability of a company. It is the result of dividing *quick assets* by the current liabilities. Quick assets include cash, temporary investments held in place of cash, and current accounts and notes receivable. The common factor among these is that each asset is readily convertible to cash, and at approximately their values shown on the balance sheet. Because inventory may not be readily converted to cash, it is the principal asset excluded from quick assets. The acid-test ratio is a measure of the extent to which liquid resources are immediately available to meet current obligations.

Tests of Solvency

Solvency refers to a company's ability to meet the interest costs and repayment schedules in connection with its long-term obligations. It differs from *liquidity*, which refers only to current obligations. The *ratio of debt* (current + long-term liabilities) *to equity capital* is useful as an indicator of the solvency of a company.

Debt capital includes both long- and short-term liabilities. It is composed essentially of cash obtained by the company through loans, bonds, or other credits on which interest or principal must be paid back on a periodic basis. From the point of view of the company, debt capital is risky. Bondholders and creditors, if not paid within the time periods of their agreements or terms and conditions, can take legal action to obtain payment, which can put a company into bankruptcy.

Equity capital, or invested money, is much less risky for the company because stockholders receive returns, yields, or dividends on their investments only at the discretion of the company's directors. Stockholders have less certainty of receiving dividends than bondholders have of receiving interest; therefore, stockholders may be unwilling to risk an investment in a company unless they see a reasonable expectation of making a higher return, perhaps through capital appreciation, than they could as bondholders.

Thus, the small business is frequently faced with the choice of finding an individual or group that will lend it some cash on which interest payments are promised at a periodic rate, or of finding investors to whom it will sell a "piece of the action," an ownership in the business.

Overall Ratios

It must be kept firmly in mind that ratios may be established for an industry. If your company is within an industry whose trade association has acquired data and published industry-typical ratios, it is useful to match your ratios against them as one measure of position. Even more important is the use of ratios in comparing your company's movement from accounting period to accounting period. Ratios will provide an immediate evaluation of your current status when compared with history.

Comparisons Are Important

If inventories are revealed to have increased 17 percent, for example, the significance is not apparent unless the change is compared with another item such as sales and working capital. Could the business really afford that much addition to inventory? Perhaps it was not so great an addition as it should have been to meet growing demand for product. Or, was the increase the result of an accumulation of unsalable goods? Individual asset and liability items must be related to something else to make their significance understandable and useful.

Key Ratios

There is a considerable difference of opinion among the "experts" as to how many ratios are key, or significant, in financial analysis. The range of possible ratios is limited only by the number and classification of accounts that are used in a business enterprise. Ratio analysis depends on simplification. Ratios tend to lose their meaning and utility when they become heavily detailed formulas. It is practicable to reduce the number of *key ratios* to ten for small-business purposes. Most of these *key* ratios derive their numerical dividends and divisors from the balance sheet; a smaller number depend on the year-end financial statement for data. The following are among the most useful ratios:

1. *Current assets to current liabilities.* This has already been discussed under the section Tests of Liquidity. The formula is:

$$\frac{\text{Current assets}}{\text{Current liabilities}} = \text{current ratio}$$

2. *Current liabilities to tangible net worth.* As with the current ratio, this is a way to evaluate the financial condition of a company by comparing what is owed to what is owned:

$$\frac{\text{Current liabilities}}{\text{Tangible net worth}} = (\%)$$

Tangible net worth is the value of a business, excluding any intangible asset items such as goodwill, trademarks, patents, copyrights, leaseholds, treasury stock, organization expenses, or underwriting discounts and expenses. In a corporation, the tangible net worth consists of the sum of all outstanding capital stock, preferred and common, and surplus, minus intangibles. In a partnership or proprietorship, it comprises the capital accounts less the intangibles. In any going business, the intangibles do have some value. However, until these intangibles are liquidated by sale so that a specific dollar worth can be identified for each item of this class of assets, it is difficult for any analyst to evaluate accurately what they might generate in a cash conversion.

3. *Turnover of tangible net worth.* This ratio shows how actively invested capital is being put to work by indicating its turnover during a specific accounting period. It is one measure of the profitability of the investment:

$$\frac{\text{Net sales}}{\text{Tangible net worth}} = (\text{number of times})$$

The ratio is not a percentage; it is rather an expression of the number of times the turnover is obtained during a given accounting period. Of course, the same accounting period must be used for both the dividend and the divisor in this formula.

4. *Turnover of working capital.* The creditor, the accountant, and the investment analyst define *working capital* as the excess of current assets over current liabilities displayed on the balance sheet. Known also as the "ratio of net sales to working capital," this ratio measures how actively the working cash in a business is being put to work in producing sales. Working capital, or working cash, is assets that can be readily converted to operating funds within a year. It does not include invested capital. The formula is:

$$\frac{\text{Net sales}}{\text{Working capital}} = (\text{number of times})$$

A business with $175,000 in current assets and $90,000 in current liabilities would have $85,000 in working capital. Most businesses require a margin of current assets over current liabilities to provide for stock, work-in-process inventory, and immediate expenses, and also to carry operating costs after the goods are sold until the receivables are collected.

5. *Net profits to tangible net worth.* As a measure of return on investment, this is one of the best criteria for evaluating forward movement, often the key measure of management efficiency. After-tax profits are usually looked upon as the payment on investment plus a source of funds available for future growth. If this return on capital is too low,

investors may consider using their capital elsewhere. Here is the formula:

$$\frac{\text{Net profits (after taxes)}}{\text{Tangible net worth}} = (\%)$$

6. *Average collection period of receivables.* This collection ratio shows how long money in a business is tied up in credit sales. To arrive at the collection period figure, calculate the average dollar figure for daily credit sales and divide this into the sum of notes and accounts receivable:

$$\frac{\text{Net (credit) sales for year}}{365 \text{ (days in year)}} = \text{credit sales per day (\$)}$$

$$\frac{\text{Notes and accounts receivable (for month)}}{\text{Credit sales per day (\$)}}$$

$$= \text{average collection period (days)}$$

Net credit sales for the year are taken directly from the annual financial statement. Notes and accounts receivable for the month are taken from the balance sheet. All receivables are included in determining the average collection period. Receivables discounted or assigned with recourse are included because they must be collected either directly by the borrower or by the lender. If uncollected, they must be replaced by cash or substitute collateral. A pledge with recourse makes the borrower just as responsible as though the receivables had not been discounted or assigned. Many managers consider a collection period excessive if it is more than 10 to 15 days longer than those stated in selling terms. "Net 30 days" is a common term for payment of an invoice. Therefore, any invoice not paid within 45 days of such a term would be considered 15 days past due, which is excessive, if not an abuse of credit.

7. *Net sales to inventory.* Known also as the "stock-to-sales ratio," this inventory turnover figure is useful in comparing one company's performance with another, or with an industry's, or internally as a figure of merit for inventory control:

$$\frac{\text{Net sales}}{\text{Inventory}} = (\text{number of times turned})$$

The "inventory" is those items intended for sale. It includes a manufacturer's finished goods, work in process, and raw material. At the resale level, it is simply the stock of merchandise offered for sale. Standard accounting practice is to value the inventory at its cost or its market value, whichever is lower. It is possible, though quite cumbersome, to calculate the inventory turns for a single item or for the entire output of a company. In multidivision companies, it is usual to calculate inventory turns on the basis of total sales within each division. This then becomes one of the measures of merit for divisional management performance. Also, it serves as a control number for corporate financial management.

8. *Fixed assets to tangible net worth.* "Fixed assets" means the sum of assets such as land, buildings, leasehold improvements, fixtures, furniture, machinery, tools, and equipment, less depreciation, of course. The ratio is obtained by dividing the depreciated fixed assets by the tangible net worth:

$$\frac{\text{Fixed assets}}{\text{Tangible net worth}} = (\%)$$

This ratio indicates how liquid net worth is by showing the relationship between investment in plant and equipment and the owners' capital. The higher the ratio, the less the owners' capital is available for use as working capital or to meet debts.

9. *Total debt to tangible net worth.* Total debt includes all obligations of the company, such as accounts and notes payable, bonds outstanding, and mortgages payable. The ratio is developed by dividing the sum of these debts by the tangible net worth:

$$\frac{\text{Total debt}}{\text{Tangible net worth}} = (\%)$$

It is important to recognize that as this ratio approaches 100 percent, creditors' interests in the business assets approach those of the owners.

10. Net profit on net sales. This is a measure of the rate of return on sales. The ratio indicates the number of cents of each sales dollar which remains after all income statement items and income taxes have been considered:

$$\frac{\text{Net profits}}{\text{Net sales}} = (\%)$$

Often the simplistic view is taken that a high rate of return on sales indicates a successful operation. However, other factors must be inspected, such as return on investment, turnover of inventory, and collections. A relatively low rate of return on sales in conjunction with a high number of inventory turns and a large sales volume may result in satisfactory earnings for a business within some kinds of industries. The recent example of the Company A supermarket operation is typical; a low rate of return on sales is acceptable in the light of other operating conditions. Net sales are gross sales minus returns and allowances and trade and quantity discounts.

Who Searches for What?

There are many more ratios that can be developed, depending on one's predilection for numbers and ability to develop confusion. It is important to recognize some of the uses to which ratios are put.

Short-term creditors such as commercial bankers, suppliers, or trade creditors are primarily concerned with the ability of a borrower to meet his current obligations on time. The ratios which are of special interest to the short-term creditor include the current ratio, acid-test ratio, and the turnover of inventory and receivables.

Long-term creditors are very much interested in the working capital position of a company as an indicator of its ability to pay interest and principal, even if earnings decline.

Management, of which you may be a part, is interested in all of the ratios described above. Comparisons of current with previous performance are made by developing ratios from previous balance sheets and financial statements. Management searches for trends rather than for absolute numbers. The ratios may be converted to graphs or bar charts in order to display these trends graphically.

Trends displayed by ratios are as important to management as is the measurement of an athlete's performance on the team. A qualitative rather than a quantitative evaluation is significant. A basketball player who scores more points than any of his teammates is desirable. But, this does not mean the other players are not performing just as well. There is more to the game than making points. So it is with evaluating a company's performance.

It would be incorrect to measure one item alone, such as return on sales or net profit. Certainly profit is the name of the game; however, the pure number, whether in percentages or in dollars, tells only a part of the story. Any one number may provide a clue to the direction in which a company is moving. Several historical numbers help complete the story and give good guidance to creditors in determining the award or rejection of a request; to investors about increasing, maintaining, or divesting their interests; and to management in making intelligent decisions for future actions, which hopefully result in continuing successful operations.

16

How Much Cash Do You Need?

IT seems paradoxical: Businesses can fail even though they own things that add up to more than they owe! It is a fact because bills have to be paid with liquid funds—cash—not with frozen assets or capital equipment. A company that runs out of cash, so as not to meet current obligations, can find itself in a critical situation, one that could lead to bankruptcy or closing down operations.

Current obligations cannot be paid off with accounts receivable, new orders, inventory, or supplies. Some of these assets can be used for the purpose of raising cash—at some cost, usually in fees or interest payments. At any rate, cash is needed to continue day-to-day operations, for the purchase of materials and goods, to pay salaries, commissions, and out-of-pocket expenses. In such cases there is no regular substitute for cash.

In times of prosperity and expansion, many managers tend to neglect cash needs. It just seems to be rolling in. So, the unintentional effect is, "Let's spend it." But there is a tomorrow that must be reckoned with. And cash is one of the best tools with which to meet tomorrow. Some managers put off studying their cash needs because it seems to be a complex and unpleasant chore. Effective cash management is neither complicated nor unpleasant. It is an essential part of successful management for both large and small businesses.

Two Kinds of Cash

Money is money. But the use to which liquid money, or ready cash, is put gives it a special label. Every business manager has to think of both kinds: *working cash* and *capital cash*. Don't become confused by the use of the words "money," "cash," and "capital" in the businessman's vocabulary. The terms "working capital" and "working cash" mean the very same thing. However, we also have "capital cash." Perhaps the latter become clearer when we call it "cash for capital expenditures."

Working cash, or working capital, is the fund from which the company draws to buy inventory, either for processing or for resale, to pay wages and commissions, to provide petty cash, and to cover all day-to-day expenses incurred in routine operations. For most companies working cash comes from the daily receipts, from checks that come in the mail in payment of accounts receivable, or from cash sales.

Capital cash is money for additions to and replacements of fixed assets such as plant equipment, tools, showcases, and other depreciable items used in the conduct of the business. Such cash may come from daily receipts in excess of working cash or from a loan of cash from a bank, individual, or creditor. If the business derives its working cash primarily from daily receipts, it is prudent to withhold the distribution of any profits in the form of cash until enough cash has been accumulated to meet the budgeted capital cash requirements.

Recognize the Differences

Many small-business owner-managers fail either to recognize or take into account the differences between working cash and capital cash. As a result, they make serious mistakes in cash management. If it weren't for the fact that it happens too often, it would be astonishing to discover that many companies in prosperous times can prove through their financial statements that they earned a big profit during the year's operations but had to borrow money to pay income taxes on the profits. For example, take the fictional DFW Construction Company.

It landed a major contract, the biggest one in four years. Gross sales increased by 60 percent above the average for the previous four years of operations. The company did a fine job, and payment was made promptly on completion. However, DFW's manager had purchased for cash all the heavy equipment to be used in this major construction job. Not a bad investment, really. The equipment would be used in later years on other jobs the company expected to bid on and win. The trouble was that all the available cash had been used to pay for the capital equipment. DFW Company had unwittingly applied all the working cash to the capital cash needs. Three months after the fiscal year ended, when taxes were due, the company had to borrow cash to pay them.

What could the manager of the DFW Construction Company have done to avoid this situation? He could have planned better, budgeted his cash outlays, *conserved his cash.* It certainly is nice to own all your own equipment but in this case it would have been wiser to lease some or all of the extra equipment needed for the immediate contract. A well-built bulldozer is no substitute for cash at payroll time, tax time—or any time.

Cash Flows in a Cycle

During the normal course of business events, cash "flows." This means that it is used to purchase materials and to pay overhead expenses. Cash pays for labor which converts the materials to salable merchandise. The sales produce receivables which become cash. The cycle is from cash to cash. It flows.

Each business has its own time cycle for the flow of working cash. Good cash management requires a knowledge of the approximate timing and amounts of cash the business needs at any point in the accounting period for any given volume of business. In planning for an adequate supply of cash, the manager must consider day-to-day needs and future increases in costs of materials, labor, and overhead.

Plan an Adequate Cash Supply

Planning for an adequate cash supply is done in the form of a budget based on forecasts and best estimates of sales and expenses. In effect, one calculates—*on a month-to-month basis*—current assets in cash income versus current liabilities in cash outlay. Figure 12 is a *cash budget,* a forecast of cash flow for the fictional ITW Manufacturing Company.

A sales estimate is the starting point. It has not been conclusively proven that anyone can infallibly foretell future events. However, it is the lot of the business manager to commit to paper his foresights or those of his supervisors. It must be done. The crystal ball has to be polished and put to use. Later on in this book we will devote space to the important subject of the techniques of sales forecasting. For the moment, assume the forecast of sales for the next 12 months is based on a projection of history tempered by knowledge of market trends and the economy.

Bear in mind that the past is merely a measuring rod. It does not take into account future plans for expansion or specific growth. The person doing the forecasting must make these special estimates and modify the historic patterns accordingly. For example, if business has grown at the rate of 7 percent per year for the past four years, it is reasonable to

Figure 12. Typical cash budget.

	ITW Company				INITIALS	›DATE
	Cash Forecast for 19____			PREPARED BY		
				APPROVED BY		

Monthly Operations	(1) January $	(2) February $	(11) November $	(12) December $	(13) Totals $
Net sales	17,500	17,500	37,500	32,500	300,000
Less: Material	8,750	8,750	18,750	16,250	150,000
Dir. labor	1,750	1,750	3,750	3,250	30,000
Overhead	2,625	2,625	5,625	4,875	45,000
Cost of goods	13,125	13,125	28,125	24,375	225,000
Gross profit	4,375	4,375	9,375	8,125	75,000
Less: Sales exp.	3,750	3,750	3,750	3,750	45,000
Gen'l exp.	1,750	1,750	1,750	1,750	21,000
Operating profit	(1,125)	(1,125)	3,875	2,625	9,000
Cash flow					
Cash bal. begin.	5,000	7,000	1,625	3,000	
Receipts – cash	22,500	17,500	30,000	40,000	
Total cash	27,500	24,500	31,625	43,000	
Less disbursements					
Trade payables	10,000	10,000	11,250	8,750	
Dir. labor	2,000	2,250	1,750	1,750	
Other mfg. exp.	3,000	3,375	2,625	2,625	
Sales exp.	3,750	3,750	3,750	3,750	
Gen. & admin. exp.	1,750	1,750	1,750	1,750	
Fixed assets add.		500		22,500	
Repay bank loans			7,500		
Total disb.	20,500	21,625	28,625	41,125	
Indicated cash short.					
Bank loans needed					
Cash bal. end.	7,000	2,875	3,000	1,875	
Material purchased	10,000	11,250	8,750	8,750	
Month-end position					
Accounts receivable	35,000	35,000	77,500	70,000	
Inventory	43,000	46,875	54,250	43,000	
Accounts payable	10,000	11,250	8,750	8,750	
Bank loans payable		2,500	50,000		

assume that, in the absence of competitive changes and with continuing market trends, a growth of 7 percent may be forecasted during the next 12-month period. If the growth toward the cumulative 7 percent is nonlinear, that is to say it is not 7 percent divided equally by 12 (months), the detailed sales records of the past four years will reveal the peak and valley months of the year, the seasonal sales cycles. These peaks and valleys then influence the sales forecast as the monthly dollar estimates are developed. It is prudent to be conservative, allowing some margin for unforeseeable events which might have a negative effect on income.

An operating expense estimate is developed next. Whether the business manufactures, retails, or wholesales merchandise, or provides a service, the rules are the same. Expenses are incurred in generating sales dollars. Calculate how much each activity of the business will cost in order to reach the sales budget. If the sales forecast shows an increase, calculate as closely as is practicable the cost increase.

For example, if raw materials cost $35,000 to produce $95,000 in sales at this time last year, and a 5 percent growth is forecast for the month's sales, it is probable that raw materials will cost at least 5 percent more this time around. (Don't forget inflation factors.) Add to this a listing of other expense items such as labor, selling expenses (including increased commissions paid for increased sales), and overheads. Department managers and well-informed supervisors should provide individual forecasts for their segments of the operations. Remember, total annual dollars are inadequate for a forecast of cash flow or cash needs. The annual forecast must be detailed *month to month.*

Some owner-managers of small businesses may want to approach this task, if it is a first-time effort, by preparing a six-month cash forecast. It may seem less tedious than having to face a 12-month crystal ball. However, when the forecast of the first six months is completed, it would be wise indeed to do the second six-month segment. A forecast of at least 12 months is essential. Many large corporations prepare cash flow forecasts month to month for the next 12 months, quarterly for the second year, and on an annual basis for three more years.

It is recognized that the further out the forecaster moves in time, the lower is his level of accuracy. However, such a long-term forecast reveals company trends in growth or decline, opportunity and risk, and indicates when it may be necessary to depend on cash from sources other than sales. It can be recognized that cash flow forecasts are especially important to corporations with monthly expenses and payrolls in multimillions of dollars. To some corporations, management of cash needs becomes a daily, rather than monthly, study.

In developing a cash budget on a month-to-month basis, a sudden peak need for cash may appear in any one month. When this is observed, it is wise to try to break that month down to a week-to-week or even a daily forecast. In this way the manager is forewarned of special problems, such as a slowdown in sales or a surge in due bills, that can result in a cash shortage. Corrective action may then be planned and executed in an effort to smooth out the uneven need for cash.

Avoid the tendency to overbuy. Inventory is not cash, but purchases of inventory must be paid for in cash. Therefore, it is important to maintain inventory levels essential to the profitable conduct of the business—no more, no less. A supplier tries as hard to sell materials and goods to you as you try to sell to your customers. Special prices and extraordinary discounts are exceptionally enticing offers made by your suppliers who perhaps have an excess of inventory and are trying to convert it to cash. Monitor your cash flow and the impact of a price-reduced overbuy on your cash flow *before* you make a commitment to your supplier. As much as possible, take advantage of trade discounts on your payables as an obvious means of reducing your cash outgo.

Avoid the temptation to overtrade. It is very difficult to resist the "carrot" of a big order offered on the condition you cut your price to the bone. But it can lead to profit disaster and a cash squeeze. It is usually better to maintain profit margins and cash income at the expense of reduced volume. At times, price competition can become so severe that it is good business sense to let your competitor take the business. Monitor cash flow and the effects of downtrading. It's a good business habit.

Separate working and capital cash accounts. Confusion can be minimized and overextensions of capital cash to the detriment of working cash can be avoided by the simple device of separating the two by means of individual checking accounts. One technique to enhance the separation and avoid confusion is to use two differently colored checkbooks. One account and color can be used for all working cash payments, and the other account and color for all capital cash expenditures. The ledgers associated with each separate account's deposits and withdrawals, if strongly followed, provide a built-in system of disciplines for cash management.

Credit and Cash Flow

Methods for controlling the cash supply should also include practices of credits which you give your customers. The business which allows customers to fall behind in their payments of invoices creates a drain on its cash balance. In effect, the business is financing the customers, often when it cannot afford to do so. Offering a discount for prompt payment, in most cases, enables a company to keep its money turning and thus operate with relatively smaller cash balances.

Cash Flow and the Billing Cycle

Some companies seem to take weeks after the merchandise has been delivered to mail appropriate invoices. Others have such tight control that the invoice arrives almost simultaneously with the goods or may be enclosed with the package. Sometimes the invoice arrives even before the goods. Guess which one most likely produces the best cash flow! In cases where an examination of the cash budget shows a temporary shortage or weakness in cash supply, re-examine the invoice timing, the billing cycle. It may be possible to shorten it. At least, it may be possible to mail the invoices the same day the shipment is made. If the package containing the goods ordered is small, obviously it is desirable to co-ordinate the cutting of the invoice document so that it can be enclosed in the package.

At times it may be necessary to borrow cash on a short-term basis to support the near-term cost of operations. Invariably, it is easier to do such borrowing when it is known ahead of time that a cash shortage is developing, according to the forecast. It is wise to discuss the forthcoming need with your banker, seeking his advice, preparing him ahead of time, learning from him exactly what information and collateral the bank might require in support of a potential loan application.

How to Develop a Cash Flow Budget

The *cash flow budget* can be compared with the balance sheet of operations. The obvious difference is that the "budget" is actually a prediction, a forecast of end-of-month finances, while the balance sheet is a historical report of financial status, usually dated at the end of a month. The forecast must involve a consideration of all elements of cash receipts and disbursements at the time they occur. It is important to make some basic assumptions in developing the budget for cash:

1. Sales will not develop evenly over the year. Therefore they must be forecast in separate monthly figures.

2. It is assumed that beginning and ending inventories for the year will be the same, because the business is a continuum of events. Of course, there will be variations in inventory levels throughout the year, and these levels will have to be forecast. Suppose the business history shows that in any month a supply is needed to support sales for the ensuing three months. Therefore, purchases of materials and labor and overhead will have to provide inventory which at each month-end will equal cost of sales for the following three months forecast. The cash expenditures for material, labor, and overhead will not relate directly to the monthly cost of sales but rather to the monthly production or receipt-of-goods schedule.

3. Assume, too, that all sales are made on terms and the

invoices are normally payable in the month following delivery. If the history of collectibles shows that the average runs about 45 days from date of invoice, despite offers of discounts for prompt payment, the impact on cash flow has to be considered. The effect is that receivables forecast each month are the result of sales made before the preceding 45 days.

4. Trade credit is available to the company, and most purchases are subject to discounts if paid for within the terms of the sale. Plan the cash budget to enable the company to take advantage of this source of income or of reduced expenses. Monthly purchases, therefore, become an integral part of the forecast of cash needs.

5. Cash disbursements for general and administrative expenses fall into the months indicated by the operating budget.

6. Any expenditures for fixed assets or capital equipment will have to be planned well in advance and reflected in the forecast.

Using these assumptions, taking inputs from your most knowledgeable aides, managers, and supervisors together with history as displayed in your well-kept records, *it is possible to predict the balance sheet for any month-end* during the year ahead.

Make Your Budget Work for You

As each month ends, record the actuals alongside the budget numbers and study the variations. Adjust your forecast during the year, and evaluate the effects on cash needs. Bear in mind that a rise in business activity can result in a temporary but significant cash shortage. Avoid the trauma of unexpectedly running out of cash, just when things "were going so well."

17

How to Determine the Kind of Money You Need

THE manager of a small business hard-pressed for cash may allow himself, without realizing it, to reach for whatever "kind" of money is handy. Actually, there are four kinds of money from which to choose, and the choice should be made according to the specific needs of the business. There are (1) trade credits, (2) short-term bank borrowing, (3) long-term borrowing, and (4) equity capital. The wrong choice made in an effort to solve an immediate problem can very well complicate the situation and put the business deeper into trouble than it already may be.

For example, the ABC Company had a significant sales increase. Within a short period of time, inventory doubled over its normal rate. ABC had difficulty collecting on the accounts receivable fast enough to meet the bills for inventory purchases. Despite the fact that suppliers extended increasing amounts of credit, cash problems increased. The

ABC manager realized that good trade credit, which enabled him to lay in large amounts of materials, was not the whole solution to successful financial management. The lesson was learned. The next time the company found itself with an opportunity to gain from a sales increase, a short-term bank loan was arranged. This took the pressure off the day-to-day operations by allowing for prompt payments of inventory purchases, which earned discounts for cash and protected the company from the jeopardies created by delayed collectibles.

On the other hand, some managers try to make short-term borrowing do the work that is better handled by long-term loans.

For example, the DEF Company needed new equipment which would cost several thousand dollars. A decision was made to arrange payment through a short-term bank loan of ten months. The reasoning was that costs of operations could be held down below normal levels, enabling the company to accumulate most of the money with which to repay the bank loan. However, problems in production, quality control, bad batches of raw materials, and employee illnesses defeated the cost reduction plan. When the bank note became due, the company had to get an extension, renew it instead of paying it off. In fact, the note had to be renewed several times at the highest interest rates.

The DEF Company learned its lesson; next time a major capital equipment purchase was to be considered, the cash flow budget would be more carefully examined and operating risks would be realistically studied along with the apparent opportunities for business growth. In this case, a long-term loan spreading payments over several years would have been the wiser choice. Every opportunity is accompanied by risks, and both have to be thoroughly considered.

Some companies try to use long-term borrowing when they really need equity capital. The GHI Company provides a good example. The company was growing rapidly, and all forecasts indicated the growth pattern would continue for at least the next three years of operations. Increased space to accommodate expansion of the production facility was truly needed to enable the company to take advantage of a real opportunity. A three-year term loan was arranged, and space was expanded to meet the need.

But other problems came along with the growth. The economy dipped, causing a cash crunch. Customers did not pay as promptly as they had before. Even major accounts which previously had taken advantage of discounts for prompt payment became collection problems, paying as much as 45 or even 60 days late. However, the bank notes could not be deferred, and the loan repayments became a severe burden. Despite the fact that business sales grew rapidly and the bank had given full support in cash advances, the need for more cash to meet more sales became an intolerable cycle.

GHI needed equity capital, not a long-term loan. It needed investors or partners who could wait longer than three years for a return on their investments, forgoing immediate dividends or interest or repayments of any kind until the company had found a reasonably sound cycle of cash flow.

Each of these businesses found itself in financial difficulty for the same reasons. Each was trying to operate at the wrong level of finance. Of course, simply preparing a cash flow budget does not assure that problems will be solved. It is imperative that the analysis of budgets and forecasts lead to the proper course of action on the part of the manager responsible for continuing profitable operations. A basic understanding of the four kinds of money is useful.

Normal Trade Credits

The use of credit is a form of short-term financing. Credit is usually granted on the company's reputation without the need for collateral and is relatively easy to arrange.

Trade credit is a practice or courtesy that businesses extend to each other. Suppliers give it each time they send materials or goods without asking for payment before or on delivery. The manufacturer extends credit when he ships finished goods to his distributors or wholesalers who, in turn, do the same for the retailers. End users of the goods often use credit, in the form of cards which verify the fact that they have a credit line, usually through a bank or some commercial collection agent. Many retail establishments operate their own credit-collection accounts for customers. All that is involved is a bookkeeping transaction. Very simple. It continues as long as terms of repayment are met by the user of trade credit.

Customer notes are another form of normal trade credit. Some banks will buy your customers' promissory notes.

Installment paper is a form of promissory note from the purchaser, who agrees to pay off the cost of the merchandise (plus an added charge for the seller's carrying the paper) in a specified number of installments over a specified period of time.

Factors offer another form of trade credit. The company sells its accounts receivable and receives cash immediately, for which it pays the factoring company a commission.

Term Bank Loans

The unsecured loan, with no collateral required, is the most frequently used form of credit for loans that are to be repaid in less than a year. Often this form of credit is used to finance accounts receivable for 30 to 90 days.

The secured loan gives money against a company's tangible assets as collateral. Accounts receivable may be acceptable as collateral. Usually, a bank will advance less than the full amount of the face value of the accounts receivable as protection against the possibility of uncollectibles. Inventory is sometimes purchased and then posted as collateral for a short-term loan; this practice is especially valuable in a business which must build inventories rapidly to meet a short, seasonal sales cycle.

Short-term borrowing refers to a loan of money to be paid back in a period of months, not longer than one year. It is usual for the lender to expect repayment of the loan, plus applicable interest, in an equal number of installments spread across the loan period at a linear rate. The loan may be secured or unsecured, depending on its amount and the lender's confidence in the borrower's ability to repay in full and on time.

Long-term borrowing is a source of money that is to be paid back over a period usually greater than one year. Loan conditions, collateral, and terms of repayment are arranged individually. Not all such loans are repaid in monthly installments. Usually, long-term loans are paid back in quarterly or semiannual installments.

Equity Capital

Money received through long-term loans and from equity capital may be used for the same purposes. Whereas long-term loans have to be repaid within a specified period of time, equity capital is money invested in the business for an indefinite period of time. The investor hopes for a return on his investment in two ways: (1) dividends or a share in the profits with no reduction in the amount of his original investment, and (2) appreciation of the equity purchase or of the money invested so that, should the share of interest acquired in the business be sold, a significant profit would be realized.

Deciding what kind of money is best suited to the need is not always easy. It is sometimes true that the business may use some of the various kinds all at the same time; for example, it may receive *trade credit* for purchases while giving it for sales, *short-term loans* to cover accounts receivable, *long-term loans* to acquire some depreciable capital equipment, and *equity capital* to finance a major growth program.

18

Do You Know
Your Sources
of Financing?

AT some point in the personal and professional career of a manager or owner of a business, he must go to the bank. Perhaps he needs a personal loan to purchase a car, or mortgage financing for a home. In managing the business, he may need an infusion of cash to support day-to-day operations or to implement an expansion program.

Anyone who has been through the experience of trying to arrange financing learns very quickly that each lending agency asks the same questions and insists on the same data: the records of financial history or P&L statement, and a balance sheet with its display of current assets and current obligations. For the personal loan, a balance sheet is prepared as part of the loan application to show tangible net worth and, in effect, working capital. And there are many questions to be answered by the business manager:

"How much do you need? For how long?

"What do you intend to use the money for?

"What terms of repayment can you meet?

"May we see your books?

"What kind of reputation do you have as a businessman?

"What kind of reputation does your company have?

"Is your industry in a phase of growth, decline, or no change?

"What are your personal habits?"

No matter from whom you are borrowing or from what source you may be seeking equity capital, the questions will follow the same pattern—probing, searching for facts, records of accomplishment. In fact, the lender or investor will be doing the same thing any manager does every day— developing information on which to base a management decision. He will be asking himself whether he should respond to or reject the loan request, invest in the company or put the capital to other use.

Typical Information Requests

Books and records. Are they up to date and well organized so that the reader can readily find the type of data useful in negotiating a finance package? What is the condition of notes payable? What is the condition and the aging of accounts payable? Are the salaries paid to the owners and other company officers reasonable? Are all taxes being paid currently? What is the order backlog? Is insurance coverage adequate? Is the head count of employees reasonable for the size of the company?

Accounts receivable. Have any of the receivables been pledged to another lender or creditor? What is the accounts receivable turnover? What is the aging of the receivables? Has a realistic reserve been set up to cover doubtful accounts? How dependent is the sales volume on one or more major accounts? What percentage of the receivables is related to the major accounts? How promptly do they pay?

Inventories. Are finished goods in marketable condition

or will they have to be marked down? How much work is in process? How much more will it take, and how long, to convert raw materials and work in process to salable finished goods? Is there any obsolete inventory or inventory for which there is no current requirement, surplus to forecast sales or production schedules? How much inventory has been shipped to customers on consignment? Will they pay for it when they sell it? Is inventory turnover in line with industry figures?

Fixed assets. What is the type, age, and condition of equipment? What depreciation policies are practiced? What mortgages or notes are outstanding against real property? How much is dependent upon conditional sales contracts? What are the plans for future growth?

Audited accounts. Have the financial statements been audited by a certified public accountant? Has the accountant provided the certification report? This states in part:

> In our opinion, the accompanying balance sheet and statements present fairly the financial position of _____ Company on December 31, 19__, and the results of its operation for the year then ended, in conformity with generally accepted accounting principles applied on a basis consistent with that of the preceding year.
>
> *(signature of accountant)*

Without such certification from a reliable auditor, few bankers, lending institutions, creditors, or investors will give much credence to a company's financial data. This is true, regardless of the financial sophistication of the company's general or financial management. In fact, a sophisticated manager, without hesitation, makes certain his control accounts, ledgers, and bank accounts are reconciled and in agreement and then willingly calls for an independent C.P.A. to audit the statements. If inventory is a significant part of the company assets, the auditor will want either to observe or to participate in a physical inventory count as part of certification.

For a company that is unable to demonstrate profitability and has inadequate or unaudited financial data, a loan of cash is unlikely. Under such circumstances any prospective investor will demand a large share of the company at a low price. On the other hand, well-organized and audited financial records of a venture which has not yet produced profits do indicate the potential for success through its knowledgeable management. Such a company will be considered for a cash loan or extended credit terms. It is highly attractive to equity capital.

A qualified independent auditor can give the top man practical help in improving operations. Having a full- or part-time bookkeeper doesn't change this fact. Further, an auditor is different from the accountant who keeps the books and draws up periodic statements. The auditor is the outside expert who checks the financial figures for reliability.

An auditor's professional opinion of the financial position of a company can be of the highest importance. The auditor's reputation and scope of service must be balanced against his charges and the business's needs. Sometimes, a small local auditor may provide just the service which suits the needs of a business whose commerce is primarily local. For multi-division, multimarket national companies, a large well-known firm of auditors may be best.

Before making a choice it is wise to talk with several different auditing firms. These interviews will provide a general idea of the attitudes, services, costs, and types of experience. More facts can be obtained from business friends, banks, suppliers, trade associations, and from local chapters of the national accounting groups.

In situations such as raising equity capital, changing the legal form of organization, and buying or selling a business, the opinion of an independent auditor should be considered mandatory. Careful thought should be given to how much, if any, supplementary accounting work on special problems the auditing firm might be asked to provide, in addition to general auditing of the records.

Lenders, creditors, and investors will also want to see the

cash budget and, of course, the sales forecast. They will want to see historic records, previous budgets versus actuals as a key to the management's ability to forecast the future with reasonable accuracy.

Ratio analysis should be provided as a measurement of the success or potential for success of the company, as well as an additional indication that management does its homework.

In the case of a publicly held company, it is requisite that earnings statements be published quarterly and full disclosures of consolidated financial operations be made annually. In closely held companies, partnerships, and sole proprietorships, there is no requirement for periodic publication of financial values. However, as part of a loan, credit, or capital investment agreement, periodic progress reports of financial operations may be required. This is a good discipline for management as well as the natural requirement which assures the lender or investor that the capital is being well handled.

Sources of Funds

There are several sources of cash and equity capital to which the owner-manager in need of cash can turn for guidance and direct aid. The most obvious of course are the *commercial banks* and *savings and loan associations*.

It is not uncommon for a *major account,* a significant customer for products or services, to finance a loan at reasonable interest rates in order to assure a continuing supply of goods. Also, a *supplier* may take the same approach to maintain a continuing consumer for his goods.

Other trade credit techniques, such as *factoring,* have been mentioned previously.

Federal government agencies are another source of financial aid for the small businessman. The *Small Business Administration,* with field offices throughout the United

States, is empowered to make financial loans at relatively low rates in several areas of commercial activity:

□ Business loans to assist small firms to finance construction, conversion, or expansion; to purchase equipment, facilities, machinery, supplies, or materials; and to acquire working capital. Loans are direct or in participation with banks.

□ Economic opportunity loans to assist small firms operated by those who have marginal or submarginal incomes or those who have been denied equal opportunity.

□ Disaster loans to assist disaster victims to rebuild homes or business establishments damaged in SBA-declared disaster areas.

□ Economic injury loans to assist small concerns suffering economic injury resulting from (1) a major or natural disaster declared by the President or Secretary of Agriculture, (2) federally aided urban renewal or highway construction programs, (3) inability to market or process a product because of disease or toxicity resulting from natural or undetermined causes, and (4) U.S. trade agreements.

□ Development company loans to assist small firms by helping to establish and finance the operations of state and local small-business development companies which make loans to small firms for equity capital, plant construction, conversion, or expansion.

□ Small Business Investment Company (SBIC) loans to assist SBA-licensed business-investment companies, which, in turn, provide equity capital, make long-term loans, and supply advisory services to small businesses.

Private financing institutions, under government guarantee, may make loans to facilitate and expedite the financing of persons and companies having contracts or engaged in operations deemed necessary for national defense. These include contractors, subcontractors, and others doing business with the Army, Navy, Air Force, Defense Supply Agency, the Interior, Agriculture, and Commerce Departments, GSA, AEC, and NASA. The lending institution applies on behalf of the borrower through a Federal Reserve

Bank to the appropriate government department or agency
for a guarantee of the loan.

The *Maritime Administration,* in Washington, D.C., may
insure construction loans and mortgages to aid in financing
the reconstruction or reconditioning of vessels.

The *Department of Agriculture,* through the Commodity
Credit Corporation, the Farmers Home Administration,
the Rural Electrification Administration, and the Farm
Credit Corporation, is involved in a number of situations
intended to aid farmers and areas dependent upon agriculture industries.

The *Department of Housing and Urban Development*
works with investors, builders, and mortgagors in arranging
housing loans and mortgage insurance, and in metropolitan
planning and development to foster good community, metropolitan, and regional planning, and the development of
low-cost housing and housing for the elderly and physically
handicapped.

The *Veterans Administration* is a source of capital for
eligible veterans. Real estate loans may be made available
for the purchase of land or the purchase, construction, repair,
alteration, or improvement of buildings to be used for the
purpose of engaging in business or pursuing a gainful operation. Loans may be available for the purchase of inventory,
equipment, machinery and for working capital to be used in
a gainful occupation.

The *Department of the Interior* has several Bureaus—
the Bureau of Indian Affairs, Geological Survey, Bureau of
Commercial Fisheries, and Bureau of Reclamation—which
are concerned with financial assistance to individuals,
partnerships, and corporate enterprises which meet the
charter requirements of the Bureaus.

The *Export-Import Bank of the United States* offers several financial programs to assist in the financing of U.S.
foreign trade. This "bank" services exporters, commercial
banks, Edge Act corporations, and overseas buyers of U.S.
goods and services.

The *Overseas Private Investment Corporation (OPIC)*

offers a variety of services to private U.S. companies interested in establishing new businesses or expanding facilities in less developed countries. These services include investment information and counseling; pre-investment and project development financing; project insurance against the risks of currency inconvertibility, expropriation, war, revolution, or insurrection; and project financing through loan guarantees and direct dollar and local currency loans.

The *Department of Health, Education, and Welfare (HEW)*, through the Office of Education and the Public Health Service (National Institutes of Health), provides loans to approved public and private schools, colleges, universities, and technical or business schools for the construction or improvement of undergraduate or graduate academic facilities.

Venture capital organizations offer equity capital and management assistance to companies in growth industries. Many of them can be located through other companies which have used their services, and through commercial-bank loan officers.

Important enough to be repeated is the fact that every one of the foregoing organizations will ask the same probing questions about a prospective borrower's financial history, present status, and plans for the future. Comprehensive, orderly records and well-conceived budgets and forecasts are among the indicators to the lender or investor that the company is operating under good management, that its probability for success is high.

PART THREE

marketing and sales

19

Forecasting Sales: Key to the Front Door

FORECASTING the future—humanity's dream of seeing what lies ahead—has been romanticized in all of the arts, literature, music, and the theatre. The fortune tellers, gazers into crystal balls, dealers of cards with secret meanings, soothsayers, witch doctors, medicine men, and mediums have become part of the folklore of every society. They specialize in probing the future for either those who will not wait and take it as it comes, those who must "know" so they can take evasive action, or those who are titillated by the notion of peeking ahead, glimpsing the goodies. People are curious; some just won't wait.

On the other hand, everything the businessman does is related to a forecast of something. There is the forecast that must be made for orders, so that sales territories can be forecast in market value, so that markets and product lives can be forecast, so that research and development can be forecast, and so that the caliber and size of the sales team can be forecast. Orders and shipments are forecast, so that factory demand can be forecast, so that materials can be forecast, so

183

that labor can be forecast, so that cash needs can be forecast, so that profits and losses and returns on investments can be forecast.

Forecasting a business has been called an uncertain, imprecise, but unavoidable necessity. The degrees of uncertainty and imprecision vary with the complexity of an organization, its markets, and its products. Think how simple, though bitter, it is for the poor blind beggar who offers a cupful of pencils to passersby. His inventory forecasts are in terms of "How many more pencils to refill the cup?" His cash forecasts are probably made daily, are based on experience and, probably, some seasonal effects such as at Christmastime, when the spirit of giving is more easily moved.

On the other hand, if the soloist beggar were to join a group of similarly handicapped people, a leader would probably be appointed. And that leader would, no doubt, prepare the forecasts for total pencil inventory and estimate cash income and outlay based on a somewhat longer time interval than "daily." Already, things are getting complicated. We can skip quickly to the larger business where, as we have learned, forecasting is essential to financial planning and to all strategic planning. It cannot be done blindly.

Who Should Forecast?

Forecasting is important enough to warrant full participation among all staff and line managers of the company, from the professional consultant to the salesman on the front line. Forecasts must be coordinated so that all the elements of available science, experience, and educated intuition can be fused into useful data.

What Makes a Good Forecast?

The quality of the people doing the forecast, especially that of the coordinator, is significantly more important than is the method used for developing the forecast. The best technical method of forecasting is not better than the flexibility and judgment of the forecaster. Good data in the hands of a person of poor judgment most certainly will result in a bad product. Bad data in the hands of a good forecaster can be adjusted to produce a somewhat more dependable product. Good data and a good forecaster are not only desirable but invaluable to the company fortunate enough to have both.

Who Should Not Forecast?

The future is rarely a straight-line extension of past experience. The business world and the economy in which it operates are dynamic. Anyone who believes that straight-line extensions of the past can prove the future should beware! He can be replaced by a sheet of graph paper, a straightedge, and a pencil. Such a person should not forecast or, if there is no way out, his forecasts should be considered mere exercises.

The Trauma of 1975

It was a bad year, far from vintage, for those who made a living doing economic forecasts. The U.S. Treasury underestimated the national deficit by almost $2.5 billion. Officials of one of the largest cities in the nation had only a vague idea of how much money they had or, more accurately, didn't have. Other states, counties, and cities periodically announced to the surprise (or resignation) of the natives that there were cash shortages, either because income was inadequate to meet forecast cash needs or because cash needs exceeded forecast income. Some people reported they had hit their forecasts on the nose. Others wanted to hit their forecasters on the nose. Few people felt comfortable with their own forecast of how high a home heating bill would be that winter.

The year 1975 was indeed filled with trauma, shock, and revelation. It is reasonable to assume that out of the poor, worse, and worst experiences of that year have come a greater attention to the value of and methodology for forecasting the "keys" to the front door of successful business management—sales.

Forecasting by Ultimatum

"Sam," says the general manager to his sales manager, "you were right on the button—give or take a few percentage points—with your last forecast."

"Thank you, boss," Sam responds in expectation of reward.

"You certainly know our market, our products, and our channels of distribution, Sam."

"Boss, it comes from hard, hard work and lots of dedication."

"Right, and because you have all these fine characteristics and because you do attain your goals, I want you to forecast a 15 percent increase for next year over this year's actuals. We need the extra business to increase our profits to make up for last year's losses!"

Sam has been given an ultimatum. Note he wasn't asked; he was told. He has a clear statement as to what his sales "forecast" is to be.

What is Sam to do? What would you do about it? Tell the boss, "No way am I going to make such a naive forecast!"? The risk is, the boss may find someone else willing to commit himself to the 15 percent increase. Win a principle and lose a job? Not many managers are so bold. The response calls for the exercise of good judgment based on experience, the first sign of a good forecaster. The proper response is to commit to an investigation that might indicate a 15 percent increase. The boss could be right.

What is called for is an intensive re-examination of all the evidence on hand, acquisition of additional evidence, market data, customer estimates, salesmen's predictions, suppliers' plans, economic indicators—all facts that prove growth or decline and that quantify the direction of sales movement. The boss could be wrong. So could you. Possibly, somewhere between his ultimatum and last year's success lies the real world of next year's volume.

Develop the data built on the best possible foundation and present the forecast to the boss. Usually the ultimatum is really a challenge calling for renewed efforts to search for growth, not a "do or die" order from the top.

So what's next?

Forecasting for Failure

It is management idiocy to exercise power and power alone to develop a forecast. Yet, some authoritarian company managers, big as well as small, pick a convenient number or one based on an impression of what the investors want to hear and assign it to the forecasters for proof. It is the lot of these poor assignees to fill in the details that "prove" the final number of the forecast. It is amazing how many times these companies do make their forced forecast come true, at least for several years in a row. But invariably things go out of control. One day there is a growing, gnawing feeling that inventories are excessive, cash isn't flowing, debts are mounting—that all the profits of the previous several years will be wiped out. The foundation upon which the financial and strategic plans were built is unsound, unrealistic.

Forecasting for Success

The first step is the accumulation of reliable historic data. This is another one of the phases of business activity that depends heavily on record keeping. Data should be detailed by model number of the product or type of service, by territories, by markets, by customers, by months, or by any other characteristics important to your particular business. Sales figures are expressed in dollars. If you are preparing a forecast for the first time, go back as far into company history as is practicable. A three-year history is reasonable. A five-year history of activity is still better. Going further back than that tends to generate a mass of data that is difficult to work with. However, if such a long history is available, skim it for evidence of severe perturbations. If there were any strong rises or dips, try to determine what caused them and judge whether or not such a recurrence of the situation is probable in the year about to be forecast.

If detailed internal figures are not available for a substantial period, consult as openly as possible with those inside and outside your company who are the most experienced, most knowledgeable in the industry. Be aware that the less historical data available to the forecaster, the greater the margin for error.

Again, avoid the hazards of the easy way out, making a forecast entirely through an extrapolation of the past—the graph paper, straightedge, and pencil approach.

Determine your share of the market in order to relate your company's sales to the total sales of the industry of which your company is a part. Do this historically; then, armed with a knowledge of your company's new-product and sales promotion plans plus some knowledge of competitive activities gleaned from field intelligence, project the next year's share of market for your company.

How to Estimate Market Size

There are two basic methods for determining the dollar share of market enjoyed by your company: the direct method and the corollary-data method.

The direct method involves the use of actual sales figures published for your industry. If you are selling nationally, census data or data published by trade publications and trade associations may be available. If your sales are regional or purely local, county and city data such as population statistics, factored by indexes of purchasing power which are calculated by trade publications or associations, are useful.

The corollary method is used when there are no sales figures available for your type of goods or services in your market area. When such is the case, it becomes necessary to estimate the volume of business by relating your sales to the sales of merchandise or services sold in conjunction with yours. An example is given by the market for tires.

If you sell or manufacture tires, you might logically determine that the sales of new cars three years ago has the prime effect on tire sales next year. Your company's historic records can be examined to assure that this pattern has held true. Again, in the absence of history, an abundance of good judgment must be used to offset the lack of actual experience. A percentage or corollary relationship can be drawn between the numbers of new cars and the number of replacement tires sold. Thus, a ratio is derived that becomes a reasonable basis for forecasting tire sales right down to types and sizes.

How to Estimate Market Share

After the total market dollars have been calculated, you are ready to determine what your share is. The percentage number for your share is derived from the formula:

$$\frac{\text{Your company sales (\$)}}{\text{Total market sales (\$)}} = \text{your company's share (\%)}$$

This formula applies to history as well as to forecasts, as long as the parameters for market sizes are observed.

Assume your company retails kitchen appliances and that you have learned through the direct method that the area you serve generated a total sales volume of $7.3 million last year. Your company sold $2.1 million of that total, so that its share was 28.8 percent. How do you project this into a forecast of the future? Population figures, household data which show specific growth or decline in your market area over the past three to five years, can be related to your company's movement. If your sales have moved at the same percentage rate as population, for example, your share of market has been holding constant. However, this does not mean things have to continue this way. A management decision can be made, plans developed, and programs implemented to cause an increased share of market to be gained by your company, either to produce an extraordinary sales increase in a growing marketplace or to hold the line at the dollar level in a declining market.

Competitive position with respect to shares of markets may be more difficult to estimate for a specific competitor than it is to estimate for the whole market or industry. In the absence of hard data, once more it becomes necessary to exercise judgment, but supported by knowledge of the competitor's products or services, pricing structure, policies, and channels of distribution from which dollar data may be estimated.

Sources of Industry Data

Useful statistical information which can be considered authoritative is most likely to be found among these sources:

Bureau of the Census. In its census of manufacturers, data may be provided for shipments in units and dollars, costs, payrolls, numbers of employees and plant facilities. Unfortunately, these census figures are aperiodically developed and published.

Department of Commerce. Reports published by the Department fill the gaps between census years with summarized data for many of the more important census classifications. Data, by industry, may be provided for manufacturers' shipments on a monthly or quarterly basis. If these reports are not suited to the direct method, they may prove valuable in the corollary data method.

Trade associations. Some companies elect to report

shipments to industry-wide associations, which, in turn, publish the data as an aggregate number for the type of component, product, merchandise, or service provided by the industry.

Trade publications. Business magazines often do market research on their own as a means of determining their own growth potentials. Some offer the reports of their research to subscribers or to those willing to purchase the reports.

National Industrial Conference Board. In its publications and releases, the NICB reviews major industries and economic developments.

Financial publications. The quarterly and annual reports of publicly owned corporations are compiled by several financial services such as Standard & Poor's and Moody's. These reports often contain descriptions of corporations' operations and brief financial data on divisional activities.

Credit reports. Credit agencies such as Dun & Bradstreet are valuable sources of information on small companies. However, when D&B reports are used, it must be remembered that the type and amount of data supplied are entirely at the discretion of the company being interviewed by the D&B investigators.

Much of the information developed by the foregoing sources is available at your public library. Make direct contact with the publishers of trade journals for specific leads on other sources. Talk with your regional directors at the nearest field office of the Department of Commerce. Visit your local chamber of commerce for local information.

Interpreting the Data

Of course, all the data obtained from the sources just described represent history, while we are interested in forecasting the future. Conclusions have to be arrived at on the basis of several critical factors of probability:

Prices may change. A forecast of more dollars next year may be the result of price increases. What about units? Purchasing and production departments have to know how many units to build, even more than they need to know the dollars. This holds true, whether or not dollars go up, down, or remain static. Therefore, forecasts must be made in units to be shipped as well as dollars.

Demand may change. Consumer interest in a product, style, or service often changes from year to year. The forecaster must be closely tuned in to such changes, predicting the point in the year when an impact, positive or negative, will be felt in orders and sales.

Judgment is subjective. The soundness of the forecast should be tested. Opinions, for that's what they really are, must be sought from salesmen, major accounts, business associates, and others whose consensus of thought is valued and, of course, who can keep confidential any company-private information revealed to them.

Economic conditions are variable. The forecaster must be aware of the best judgments of economic authorities and must keep up to date on what is happening to the economic health of the nation. In times of recession, luxury items may decline in sales. When fuel shortages threaten, sales of full-size automobiles tilt downward in favor of the smaller vehicles, which get more miles per gallon. However, sales of service and maintenance materials may increase in hard times as people make every effort to extend the useful life of equipment.

Accuracy of Forecasts

The long-range forecaster, one who has to estimate a demand five, ten, 15 or more years into the future, can anticipate a lower degree of accuracy at the 15-year period than at the five-year interval. Similarly, the annual forecaster is often quite accurate 30 days out, less at 90, and still less accurate as the months wear on into the forecast period.

Rolling the Forecast to Maintain Accuracy

A technique used by many who are responsible for fore-casting orders, which convert to sales, over a one-year period is known as the *rolling forecast*. It is one very acceptable method for maintaining a relatively high degree of midterm accuracy. Its adaptability to a specific company depends very much on the flexibility of the procurement/production cycles and lead times. A simple format for the rolling fore-cast is illustrated in Figure 13. Separate forecasts are pre-pared for units and dollars.

A typical application would be in developing the initial forecast of orders for the year ahead. It may be prepared by a company's salesmen, its manufacturers' representatives, or its distributors. Where a field sales organization is in opera-tion, it is usually prepared by the salesman or manager re-sponsible for a territory or region, who takes inputs from individual sources and assembles them as a "regional fore-cast." Where a multiple number of regions comprise the total market, the individual regional forecasts are combined into a "national forecast," "overseas forecast," and so on.

Detail is provided for each model, or style, or color—depending on the level to which a forecast must be made and to which the organization is capable of forecasting—for each of the first three months of the forecast. Then each of the three succeeding quarters are forecast (not separated into monthly periods) to provide a full 12-month cycle. This method may be extended to include the next six-month seg-ment to provide an 18-month forecast; or a 12-month seg-ment, for a two-year forecast. However, it would be more appropriate to refer to such an extension as an "estimate" (or "guesstimate") rather than a "forecast" of orders.

The individual forecast data sheets are then delivered to the company's forecaster for consolidation, calibration, and confirmation. The company's forecaster may indeed be the owner or the general manager or the marketing, product, or sales manager. Whatever the title may be, the function de-

Figure 13. Format for the rolling forecast.

Orders ☐ ☐ Sales
Units ☐ ☐ Dollars

Region _____
Prepared by _____

Period Beginning _____ 19 ___

Period Beginning _____ 19 ___

| Model No. | First Quarter (Q1) | | | Q1 Total | Q2 Total | Q3 Total | Q4 Total | Total 12 months | Q1+Q2 Total | Q3+Q4 Total | Total 12 months |
	Month 1	Month 2	Month 3								

mands that the responsible person be experienced, knowledgeable, and capable of exercising good judgment.

To maintain an optimum level of accuracy for the near-term forecast, the forecast is revised or updated every three months. The three months just completed are dropped from the forecast; what had been the second quarter now becomes the first quarter and is detailed by month, while a new quarter is added to the forecast.

Conversion from *orders* to *sales* is a mathematical extension of the data. This requires an intimate knowledge of the materials procurement and production events that lead to shipments. Of course, if delivery is uniformly 45 days after receipt of order (ARO), for example, the conversion of the data to a sales forecast is a matter of simply changing the dates at the top of the columns of the form. It is seldom a simple mathematical conversion. Except in the case of a one-man organization or in the case of a company that is exclusively a marketing-selling organization without manufacturing responsibility, it is unusual for the same person to forecast both orders and sales. The requisite knowledge is usually quite different for each of the two types of forecasts.

Targets Are Needed

Although it may be management idiocy to use executive power to force a forecast, it is important for management to establish goals against which forecasts are to be developed *to determine validity of the goals.* The goals, or targets, may be expressed in terms of gross margin profit or sales. These numerical factors are interdependent; one can be derived from the other. The flexibility referred to earlier comes into close play in developing the final forecast. Each of the separate forecasts, orders, sales, expenses, costs, cash, profits, is fine-tuned or adjusted up to the last moment, when management gives its blessing. Management, in turn, must be flexible enough to adjust goals to meet the realities of the situation.

The forecasts, on acceptance by management, become known as "budgets." The budgets are the official targets for financial and strategic operations. Programs which enable the budgets to be met or exceeded are developed and implemented by the organization at the staff and line levels. Bear in mind that in many small businesses there are no clear-cut distinctions between "staff" and "line."

The sales manager may also be the field sales organization. The marketing manager and the production manager may also be the president or the owner. There are no rigid rules for management organization. The organization chart, if one has been published, usually reveals titles. Functions certainly vary from company to company, business to business. No matter.

What does matter in forecasting is the caliber of the people who make the *initial input* to the forecasting process. This usually means the caliber of the people who are in direct contact with the company's customers. Again, ignore the title. Let's call the company's representative who stands in front of the customer, by telephone or in person, a "salesman." And, because his forecasts are so important to successful business planning, it is well worthwhile to devote some pages to a discussion of the function of selling.

20

How to Select, Train, and Motivate Good Salesmen

THE impression a customer gets from a salesman's actions is the impression which that customer will have of the company. The actions of a salesman can bring to a positive, profitable conclusion all the advertising, promotional, and public relations efforts of the company, or they can vitiate all that hard work.

The job of representing to the customer all of the people, products, and energies that have brought the company to its present level is a crucial one. A misfit can tarnish a company's reputation, alienate customers, and create a multitude of internal problems. One of the most important personnel jobs a manager can do for his business is to make every effort to weed out misfits already on the job and to bar the door to any potential problem-makers. How well can he do it? Probably with some degree of success and some measure of failure.

The profession of selling is considered to be among the most individualistic and creative skills. And, because of this, the most experienced recruiter, owner, general manager, sales manager, is bound to find some failures among the many successes. Every supervisor of a sales team has stories to tell about the problems he had with Harry, to offset the good times with fantastic Frank.

No manager can weed out all of the misfits among the career salesmen. The best he can hope for is a continuing job of improving his batting average. There are programs that can increase the probability of achieving a high batting average. They begin with selection, go on to training, motivation, and rewards that can build high performance and can keep the achieving salesmen on the team.

Write a Job Description

Don't "talk" a job description. There are many opportunities for misunderstanding when two people engage in a conversation and one tries to describe to the other the kind of person who makes a good salesman for the specific company. *Write* the description so that people who can help find potential candidates will more likely comprehend exactly what the job is all about and what persons are best suited to it.

Selling for one company is *not* the same as selling for another. One company's products may be highly technical. The buyers may very well be engineers of high sophistication. When such customers meet salesmen, they want to talk technical data, design, specifications, and benefits, even before they get to price and delivery. Obviously, the salesman for this kind of product and its company—manufacturer, rep, or distributor—must be able to meet the customer at his own level, if talk is to be converted to a purchase order.

On the other hand, if a purchasing agent intervenes between the engineer and the salesman, it may not be necessary for the salesman to be able to talk fluently in engineering language; a proposal specification or data sheet may be adequate. Or, if the product is a relatively uncomplicated off-the-shelf consumer item, personality and the ability to think on his feet may be among the most important characteristics of the salesman candidate. Where fluency in technical language is a must, an engineering degree or at least some technical education may be a requirement for potential salesmen. In less technical selling situations, academic education may not be as important as other elements, such as appearance and a glib tongue.

Because the requirements of a selling job may range widely, it behooves the manager who wants to improve on his batting average to spell out the duties and responsibilities of the position. This description should define the type of selling. Does the company sell a product, a service, or a combination of the two? What are the channels of distribution? Will the salesman call on end users, distributors, retailers, house accounts, or a combination? Say so. Who does the salesman report to in the company? What is the method of compensation: straight salary, straight commission, salary plus commissions and bonuses? Will expenses be reimbursed, or will there be an expense account? Will a company car be furnished, or will the salesman use his own? Policies? Practices? And, of course, what past experience is considered minimal for the salesman?

Select the Self-Starter

Salesmen often have to work without direct supervision. Initiative and perseverance are desirable characteristics. How much of a self-starter is needed depends on the job to be done. If the salesmen check into the office or work at the office every day, it is relatively easy to review briefly the accounts and the plan for the day. If the salesmen are truly field operators, perseverance and initiative are most important to the vitality of the sales effort.

Look for Reliability

Salesmen often work alone. Their managers cannot always be with them. Therefore, the individual salesman must be reliable, trustworthy, and able to gain the confidence of his customers. The ethical behavior and integrity of the salesman is difficult to predetermine. Here it is wise to check references. Talk with his past employers and, if possible, with some of the accounts he has called on.

Seek Mental Ability

The intelligence level needed for successful selling varies with the demands of the assignment. Some jobs can be performed by memorizing a canned sales pitch. Others require a comprehensive knowledge of products and services, and of the customers who might use them. Make certain the mental capacity of the candidate salesman matches the requirements of the job.

Ask about Willingness to Travel

If the applicant doesn't know how much travel is required, describe exactly how much time he is expected to spend in travel, especially if it calls for overnight trips. Does his wife object to his absence on business? If so, be aware that personal problems can arise between the man and his wife that could seriously affect performance.

On the other hand, be aware that, for whatever reason, some salesmen are overly eager to travel. Perhaps it is because they enjoy the big welcome and the attention they get on their return from a trip. It may be necessary to apply some controls on such salesmen's travel, to make certain each trip is necessary.

Describe the Person

Whether or not it becomes part of the job description is not important, but it is critical to success to put down on paper a detailed description of the personal traits and behavior characteristics of the individual who typifies in the mind of management a desirable member of the sales team.

Don't choose a salesman because he is reported to control some accounts. Such a person is always available to the highest bidder, even if it is fact (and it rarely is) that he can bring substantial sales with him to his new employer for a fast start.

Don't pick a salesman for his trade secrets. This type of person, too, is usually available to the highest bidder. You may not be able to hold on to this Benedict Arnold. After he has learned your secrets, there may be nothing to stop him from moving again to a competitor of yours. Many companies have successfully brought legal action against competitors, charging misuse of trade secrets or other information gained by the employee while working for and being paid by his former company.

Don't expect miracles or sudden results from a new salesman. No matter how experienced he is, he must become familiar with your routines, policies, and practices and, of course, with your products and services.

Don't expect the salesman to be a top achiever *without* support from his company in the form of periodic training, and motivation techniques.

Who Needs Training?

Sales training is often thought of as being applicable only to new salesmen. However, training is a continuing requirement from the time a salesman is new through the time he is considered experienced. Depending on how the word "new" is used, a "new salesman" (that is, a "recent addition" to the sales department) can fit any one of the following categories:

- He is new to selling as well as to the company's products or services.
- He has prior selling experience, but not with this company's products or services.
- He knows the company's products and services but has no previous selling experience; possibly he transferred into sales from another activity within the company.
- He has selling experience with the company's type of products and services, gained from employment with another company in the same industry.

A training program that satisfies the needs of all four of these categories is essential. There is a subtle objection to the word "training." Perhaps it is because no one likes to be "trained" to do anything—"training" is usually applied to so-called dumb animals. "To deliver a learning experience" is a better term than "training," no doubt. However, it obviously makes for awkward sentences. "Teaching" may also be less objectionable than "training," but it too tends to be awkward. Therefore, we will abide by the current practice and refer to the "training program." There should be a minimum of three phases to such a program:

1. *Company policies* dealing with, for example, credit, minimum order size, delivery, shipping methods and costs, and returns and allowances must be exposed to the salesman. He must be made familiar with procedures for order processing, and activity and expense reports; he must know exactly when details are expected of him and what details are needed to account for time and expense. What he can't do is just as important as what he can do. For example, if he has no authority to negotiate price without prior authorization, he must be made fully aware of that fact so that embarrassment with a customer may be averted.

2. *Product information* must be provided, orally and in written form. Catalogs and price sheets; technical data;

proposal formats and specifications; and operating, service, and maintenance manuals should be given to him for reference and study. Competitive product and price information should also be developed and included in the training package. Invariably, a salesman who thoroughly knows his product and that of his competitors is a more confident, more effective salesman, welcomed more readily by customers for the technical help he is able to provide.

3. *Selling techniques,* specifically related to composite knowledge of the industry, customer benefits, how to open and how to close an order, must be shared with each of the salesmen. Selling is a dynamic profession. New ways of doing an old job are always being developed. "Old dog" salesmen are often among the most willing to learn new tricks. Often they make excellent informal instructors for the "young tigers." Invite the more successful among the older men on the team to share their advanced knowledge and experience during the training programs. Much can be learned from them about the "one that got away" or the "biggest sale I ever made."

It is possible to purchase packaged training programs with instructors' guides. These can be used by the salesmen either in teams or as individuals, each moving at his own pace. However, a time limit should be specified so the training program is utilized by all. Training programs are available in written form, in audio cassettes, on video tape, motion picture film, slides, and filmstrips. These programs, however, are general in nature and usually deal only with selling techniques.

If there is no one in the company either qualified or with adequate time to prepare a specialized training program, it is possible to purchase the services of training specialists who will tailor-make programs to fit the company's specialties. Many organizations offer sales-training seminars which travel to major cities throughout the country. On a selective basis, there are advantages to sending the salesmen to these seminars when they are scheduled for a city near the home base.

Field Sales Supervision Is Valuable Training

As an ongoing part of the sales-training program, it is important for the boss to make sales calls with each of the salesmen, whether or not it requires out-of-town travel or can be done in the headquarters city. On these sales calls the salesman should carry the initiative.

After each sales call, or at the end of each day, there should be a frank *but positive* talk, pointing out what was done right and which areas could use improvement. Try to get the salesman himself to point out the areas where he feels improvement could be and will be made. Above all, salesmen need encouragement, *not* criticism. The amount of time that must be spent with an individual salesman is indicated by his level of achievement.

More Bookkeeping—Sales Records

The new salesman should be given—or, in a new territory/start-up situation, be assisted in creating—a list of accounts and prospects. The format best suited to the job is the one with which the salesman feels most comfortable. There are no rigid formats. However, because of changing times, it is recommended that loose-leaf notebooks be used, large or pocket-size.

The salesman should be given as much history as is available on the orders in units and dollars for his accounts. Knowledge of the traits, likes, and dislikes of the customers should be shared along with details of customers' organization charts which indicate those who are influential in the buying or specifying process.

Once he has been supplied adequately with history, it is incumbent upon the salesman to maintain his own records. He should be made aware of how his supervisor will maintain his equivalent records so that, when the salesman's records are audited or should questions arise as to any specific orders or dollars written, there will be no "language barriers" or misunderstanding in communications.

Sales Meetings Are Training Opportunities

Too often a sales meeting becomes a lecture platform for the boss. It is important that the boss talk *with* his salesmen, not just *to* them. He, too, must be willing and able to listen as well as to speak. Sales meetings are excellent occasions for inviting the purchasing agent of a key customer to speak to the group about what he looks for in a salesman. Reps, distributors, or dealers, too, can fulfill a similar function and would probably be flattered by such an invitation.

Rather than run the sales meeting continuously by himself, the boss should assign the direction of specific segments of the meeting to others in the company. The credit manager could valuably spend some time describing credit and finance and answering questions from the floor; the production manager could describe programs for improving quality or for shortening the delivery cycle; the general manager or owner could describe the company's plans for growth and expansion; and so on. Some of the more articulate salesmen should be assigned responsibility for leading parts of the meeting in discussions about problems in and solutions for selling specific products or types of customers.

And don't forget to review or preview the company's advertising, sales promotion, and public relations programs. Salesmen are especially interested in how staff functions are being programmed to help them in the field.

Enthusiasm Is Infectious—and Essential

Enthusiasm is an essential ingredient that must appear with sincerity in a salesman's speech and manner. Certainly some people seem to radiate enthusiasm, shine with natural vigor, while others seem quite restrained and inhibited.

No one expects a salesman to be a Pollyanna. Now and then, like anyone holding a job, salesmen feel discouraged. And, because they are usually articulate, they gripe a lot when they feel let down. A salesman who loses his enthusiasm can rarely hide it, but a salesman with enthusiasm for his job, for his catalog of offerings, for his company is certain to pass it along, infect his prospects and customers with the same positive feeling.

Maintain the Spirit

Assuming the company has a continuing training program which keeps the sales force well informed on policies, products, and selling practices, how does the manager keep his salesmen smiling, keep them selling? There are two broad categories of techniques for motivating—another word for "stimulating"—the sales force: financial and inspirational.

What Are Financial Motivations?

Dollars, of course, are compensation and physical rewards for good performance. This can mean commissions on top of base salary, bonuses, profit sharing, prizes, and salary increases.

Dollars, financial rewards for achievement, are among the most important builders of enthusiasm in the professional salesman. As an example, let's look at what occurred in a small manufacturing concern which sold its products throughout the United States through eight field salesmen. The vice president for sales of this company developed a compensation plan which he sincerely expected to motivate the salesmen to new, higher order-writing levels.

Quotas were established for each of the men, varying according to the forecasts for each of the territories. When each man reached 50 percent of his quota for orders, he participated in commissions. He received 2 percent commission on every dollar he wrote between the 50 percent and the 100 percent quota levels. For every 5 percent increment over quota he received 0.5 percent commission. Beyond the 110 percent point he received no commissions.

The vice president for sales was sure the plan would succeed; it didn't. Why? There was no incentive for anyone to go beyond quota. In fact, there was an excellent reverse incentive, one that might cause the salesmen to defer new orders, once they had made quota, sliding them into the next quota period where they could be applied to quota performance and could help earn the 2 percent commission rate.

The lesson was learned. The commission structure was changed to provide an incentive for the salesmen to maximize, without any ceiling, the order dollars within any one quota period. The new incentive plan promised 0.5 percent for the first 50 percent of quota achievement, 1 percent for the next 25 percent achievement, 1.5 percent for the final 25 percent level up to the 100 percent completion of quota commitment. Without ceiling, 2 percent commission was paid on all orders written above the quota level within the same quota period.

It worked. The salesmen sold enthusiastically to make their quotas quickly so they could participate in the maximum commission payments. There was no reason at all to defer orders, or "sandbag," as it is put in the salesman's vernacular. There was every reason to get orders into the office as soon as possible, certainly before the calendar closed a quota period.

If you feel it is necessary to put a ceiling on a salesman's earnings, make it a high ceiling. Enable him to earn in accordance with his willingness to work and the results he produces.

Sales contests and *special incentive programs* are very popular and should be timed to cause extra selling efforts in times when inventory levels are high and it is desirable to generate an extraordinary input level of orders, for cash flow reasons, for example. Awards for winning can be given in either money or merchandise. Many times, assuming the merchandise is substantial and highly visible—a boat, a car, a camera—merchandise is preferred because the winner feels he gains greater recognition in the eyes of his peers and his family as he walks off with the booty.

Avoid the all-or-nothing kind of contest in which there is only one winner, one prize. In such a contest, the man who has always been the top salesman may walk off with the only prize; other good men on the team will feel cheated and resentful. The next contest will not produce the desired effect. Do offer a series of prizes against attainable goals. For example, award first prize to the man who produces the greatest percentage of dollars beyond quota, the second prize to the next achiever, and so on, for at least three awards.

Does it sound like salesmen respond to money? Why not? They talk price, discounts, money, payments, terms—money all day long. Of course they respond to money. Isn't that an important way a salesman's performance is measured? His job is to close orders which are totaled in dollars and accumulated against a quota expressed in dollars. Although units may also be part of the quota, this is done in an effort to control product mix. Fortunately for their employers, salesmen are sensitive to dollars—and to other rewards.

What Are Inspirational Motivations?

Money is important to salesmen, but it isn't everything. As with most people, salesmen need recognition. Money is one form of recognition, but there are others that matter.

There are scrolls, diplomas, and plaques for special achievement—"salesman of the month," "salesman of the year." Lapel pins and tie tacs are items of pride when they show that Salesman John has been with the company five, ten, or 25 years. When such awards are made, send letters to his customers and to the local papers. Brag about how proud the company is of John. Great for his ego. "Food" on which his enthusiasm will feed for quite some time.

Dinner with the boss, including the salesman's wife, makes the achiever feel and look important to his family. A special reward for a job well done—an invitation for an expense-paid trip to the plant for a specially conducted tour or a vacation weekend for two, for example—fires the enthusiasm, makes the salesman feel that he is part of the company, and inspires him to even greater achievements against the new quota.

Some companies have special achiever clubs to which a salesman is appointed automatically on the attainment of specific goals. For example, the "million dollar" circle recognizes insurance salesmen who have written a million dollars worth of insurance. They are the elite!

Does It Sound Expensive?

Any program costs money. Wisely spent on a well-conceived plan, the outlay can yield financial benefits to the company. Programs which offer financial, merchandise, and special holiday prizes, commissions, bonuses, and other special incentives should result in increased orders which convert to sales which convert to profits! Inspirational awards are long-term investments in building and maintaining morale and the enthusiasm which is so desirably infectious.

21

How the Professional Salesman Manages Time and Territory

THERE are three major operating problems facing sales managers and salesmen.

Problem 1—The salesman's average day. The average industrial salesman spends 45 percent of his time traveling and waiting, 19 percent doing clerical work, and only 36 percent selling. Additionally, 65 percent of all sales calls are made to the wrong people, and 75 percent of all orders are written by 25 percent of the salesmen. The average salesman is not spending enough time selling and should try to convert some of his traveling and waiting time into selling time.

Problem 2—Selling existing accounts. Not only do salesmen spend only one-third of their day selling, but the average salesman spends too much time calling on marginal and medium-yield accounts. About 80 percent of the accounts produce only 20 percent of the total revenue. The salesman could substitute a planned telephone call in place of some of his premises visits without losing sales volums and, consequently, recover sales time that can be re-employed elsewhere, more productively.

Problem 3—Total market coverage. The average salesman is so busy selling existing customers (large, medium, and small) that he doesn't have enough time to contact the potential market. However, the salesman's time is already overloaded. He just hasn't the time or the knowledge to set up a thoroughly planned, well-organized new-account program. A *U.S. News and World Report* article gave these reasons why customers quit buying:

  1 percent die
  3 percent move away
  5 percent because of friendships with executives or salesmen in other companies
  9 percent because of competition
 14 percent because of product dissatisfaction
 68 percent because of *no contact* with, the *indifference* of, or the *attitude* of salespeople

Telephone If You Can't Go

Almost every service or product that can be imagined can be sold by telephone. Skeptics say, "Our line can't be sold by telephone. A personal interview is absolutely necessary." Well perhaps. But the facts are that a large percentage of salesmen merely take orders on their premises visits. In many cases, these orders could be taken by telephone or by mail.

The telephone is not always as effective as a customer visit. However, it is the next important medium of customer contact. Like the visit, it provides two-way communication. It injects personality into sales narration. But, and this is important, it also makes possible many more sales contacts per unit of sales time. And at lower sales costs! More prospects exposed to the product in less time, more contacts, broader market areas.

Let's take a look at account cycling. This simply means contacting a customer at the time when he is most likely to be ready to buy. Another way of saying this same thing is, cycling sales calls according to the customer's inventory levels.

The secret of successful account cycling is (1) keeping a simple record of each account, on which is indicated its usual buying times or intervals, and (2) arranging these accounts in proper date sequence and having a method of contacting them at the proper time.

The two most effective ways of account cycling contact are face-to-face visits and telephone contact. It is axiomatic that 100 percent face-to-face can be rejected as being impractical. A more practical method is account cycling by telephone, supplemented by face-to-face visits. In some cases, such as with marginal accounts, the telephone might virtually replace face-to-face visits. In others, as with prime accounts, telephone calls could supplement regular premises visits.

Planning Pays Off

A professional salesman carefully plans his sales time. He doesn't waste it or spend it without a plan but *invests* it in a way that produces maximum return. Intelligent planning can reduce the time taken by nonselling tasks; for example, good routing will reduce travel time; appointments or advance notification by telephone to customers will reduce waiting time; effective, planned telephone use on a regular basis to customers will greatly reduce the number of face-to-face visits required.

A salesman can make only a limited number of sales calls per year. In order for him to get the maximum return for each sales call he invests, it is necessary that he allocate his calls among big customers and little ones, big prospects and little ones. A salesman should begin by analyzing his own records of calls and sales to customers and prospects, particularly the history of sales to an account in terms of (1) dollar volume, (2) number of calls, (3) nature of calls, (4) length of calls, and (5) profit potential.

A salesman's next step should be to set a sales target for each customer and prospect based on his knowledge of the customer and his territory. He should recognize that his company's goal is not just volume, but net profit. One way to set a sales target is to set a target for a product or a territory and then break it down by accounts.

The purpose of a sales target is to assist the salesman in allocating his time and planning his calls. Target setting cannot be based purely on statistics and mathematics; it involves a lot of intangible factors, such as judgment of customer, products/services, and territory.

After the salesman has carefully established his sales target, his next step is to develop a sales call budget. The first thing the salesman should do is to calculate the total number of sales calls he has available to allocate to customers and prospects. For example, if a salesman averages four contacts per day, he multiplies this figure by the average number of working days per year (225) and comes up with an availability of 900 calls per year.

The next step is to set up a call frequency based upon the type of selling and the profit potentials of the accounts. Customers and prospects should be grouped into a few basic classifications, according to the frequency with which it is valuable to call them. A salesman will find that he will want to see some accounts quite frequently, some less frequently, and others only occasionally.

It is recommended that salesmen apply the following general principles in classifying accounts and determining call frequencies.

A *(large) accounts* are those to call on most frequently, such as once a month.

B *(medium) accounts* are those to call on about half as often as the A accounts, such as once every two months.

C *(small) accounts* are those to call on about one-fourth as often as the A accounts, such as once every four months.

Each month the salesman should telephone the B and C accounts that are not on that particular monthly call cycle. The use of the telephone as a marketing tool will enable a salesman to cycle his customers on a monthly basis. In these cases telephone contacts can be just as effective as premises contacts.

As a rough rule of thumb, figure 15 percent of the accounts will fall into the A category, 25 percent into the B classification, and the remaining 60 percent into the C classification.

At least once a year, the professional salesman reviews the classifications of each account and changes the classifications where necessary.

Going hand in hand with all of the foregoing is setting up a routing system: a travel plan or itinerary. To accomplish this, the salesman takes a map of his territory and marks on it the location of every customer and prospect, using a different color to designate each classification of account. This enables him to set up a profitable and a time-saving routing system.

Next, using his map, he experiments with various possible routings until he has selected the best one. He finds that, depending upon the size of his territory, each loop, or trip, covers part of a city or several cities. In planning a trip, he will want to make sure that he (1) covers all loops every call cycle, (2) calls on every A account (prospect or customer) face to face, (3) calls on half of the B accounts face to face and telephones the other half, and (4) calls on one-fourth of the C accounts face to face and telephones the other three-fourths.

Salesmen will be able to use the time saved in many other areas, such as upgrading low-producing customers, introducing and demonstrating new products, and assisting customers with displays.

Key Town

Key-town operation involves establishing a route for the salesman-on-the-road to follow. Key towns are regular stopover points. All other surrounding towns are telephoned from the nearest key town.

Skip Stop

Skip stop is a modification of key town. More than one group of key towns is involved. The salesman takes one route the first trip out; the other route the next trip. During each trip he telephones to towns he doesn't plan to visit.

The best plan depends upon a salesman's organizational setup, size of territory, and methods of travel. Effective implementation depends upon the availability of telephone facilities and suitable working arrangements at each town. Hit-and-miss calling will prove nonproductive. A salesman *must* plan and schedule time in order to telephone. Hotel rooms having "guest dialing" are most popular with salesmen who travel.

Under suitable conditions, a self-motivated salesman who plans and manages his time and territory, using the telephone, key town, or skip stop, will find that he will have more time to: (1) contact more customers, (2) locate new customers, (3) qualify prospects, (4) sell face to face, and (5) increase sales. Calling on everyone with equal frequency is a poor investment of time and energy.

A good professional salesman is as skilled in managing himself as the successful general manager is in managing his total operations.

22

How to Understand
Sale and
Payment Terms

EVERY purchase, every sale has some sort of term, or period, for payment and a set of conditions pertaining to the exact amount of money due the seller. The simplest term and conditions occur in the over-the-counter sale in a retail establishment. The "term" is immediate payment, through cash or credit card, on receipt of the merchandise. "Conditions" are the exact amount appearing on the label, with no further discount allowed. Terms of sale and payment are not necessarily alike for any two trades or industries. Even companies in the same business may have different terms. As a result, a businessman may become confused and spend an inordinate amount of time figuring out the meaning of the terms of sale quoted on merchandise or materials he buys.

Discounts and invoice terms can be divided into two broad classes: terms of sale and terms of payment. *Terms of sale* set forth the conditions under which the goods are sold.

They specify quantities and prices plus trade, quantity, and seasonal discounts offered to the buyer. *Terms of payment* specify the conditions under which the buyer is expected to make payment: cash discount, anticipation discount, and any penalties which may be imposed for late payments.

Discounts Are Normal Practices

A *trade discount* is a reduction in price (calculated from published suggested end-user prices) given by a manufacturer to wholesalers and retailers. Discounts vary for each of these groups; therefore, they are sometimes referred to as "functional discounts." A trade discount may be a single percentage reduction, or a series of percentage reductions, such as 30 and 10 and 5 percent. Trade discounts are supposed to cover normal expenses of the different functional groups and still yield a reasonable profit margin each time the goods are resold. The major disadvantage of trade discounts is that they do not enable direct comparison of prices quoted by different sellers without knowledge of the list or other resale price on which the discount is based.

Figuring the dollar value of trade discounts calls for simple arithmetic. Assume you are a retailer and a product you want to carry for sale has a suggested end-user or list price of $49.50 with trade discounts of 30, 10, and 5 percent. The cost to you is calculated this way:

List price	$49.50
Less 30%	14.85
	34.65
Less 10%	3.47
	31.18
Less 5%	1.56
Your cost	$29.62

Your cost per item is $29.62, and, if you sell at list price, the product will yield a gross profit margin of $19.88. The aggregate of these separate discounts is the equivalent of a single discount of 40.2 percent. Why not just give a 40.2 percent discount and be done with it? The discount structure is broken down to several layers to enable the vendor to include extra discounts for a variety of reasons, such as accepting immediate delivery, buying a specific package or mix of merchandise, or for special price promotions. There are no rigid rules. A discount structure might have only one or two levels instead of the three given in the example.

Quantity discounts are used by sellers to encourage customers to buy in larger quantities. A quantity discount may be applied to an entire order. The discount may be related to specific breakpoints of quantity ordered:

Units ordered	Discount from prevailing list
1 to 24	30%
25 to 49	35%
50 or more	40%

Many manufacturers of consumer merchandise pack their products in standard boxes containing a specific quantity of the items. It is a normal practice to offer one discount for an order of a standard pack, and a lower discount for any smaller quantity.

Discounts may be offered in merchandise, for example, "Order ten, get one extra at no charge." Of course, conditions of the Robinson-Patman Act must be observed with respect to price differentials.

Seasonal discounts or early-order discounts may be offered to the buyer who agrees to take delivery of the goods in advance of the normal or seasonal buying period. It is an incentive to buy earlier than is really necessary from the purchaser's view.

Terms of Payment May Vary

Prompt payment discounts or *cash discounts* are offered to buyers for payment of an invoice within a specified time period. A prompt payment benefits both the seller and the buyer. Obviously, the added discount tends to increase the buyer's profit margin by having the effect of reducing the net purchase price. The seller benefits by improving his cash flow, reducing the credit risks on collections, reducing the reserves for bad debts, and increasing the rate of capital turnover, which makes it possible to operate the business on less capital than would be required if customers paid late.

Cash discounts offered for prompt payment of invoices vary from business to business. Cash discounts are always related to *number of days* in which the payment must be made, dated from shipment of goods or from date of invoice or from date of receipt of goods. Assume you have an invoice dated June 2 for $1,000 and it carries terms of "2/10, net 30." This means that if you pay the invoice within ten days or by June 12, you may deduct 2 percent from the invoice and remit $980. If you pay between 11 and 30 days after the date of the invoice, you must pay the full amount, $1,000. The effect is that you save 2 percent by paying within ten days. This is equivalent to a yearly rate of 36 percent interest. At times it pays to borrow from the bank on a short-term basis to take advantage of a number of invoices which offer cash discounts; the borrower can pay the interest on the loan out of the savings from these cash discounts and still have some money left over. Here are some discount rates in common use for prompt payment of invoices, and their equivalent annual rates of interest:

1/10, net 30:   18%/year
2/10, net 30:   36%/year
3/10, net 30:   54%/year

Anticipation discounts are sometimes offered to buyers for advance payment of invoices which have due dates. There are no apparent uniform policies for anticipation discounts. Some firms allow it, while others state on their invoices, "No anticipation allowed." This type of discount is usually negotiated between the buyer and seller.

Interest charges may be applied to invoices which are

not paid when due. This is, in effect, the reverse of anticipation discounting. It is common practice to provide an advisory of late charges on the invoice. A rate of 1½ percent per month, or an effective annual interest rate of 18 percent, is the norm. It is intended to encourage buyers to pay their bills on or before the end of the "net" date. Whether it has this effect in practice is questionable. If the seller cannot collect the face amount of an outstanding bill when it is due, he will certainly have difficulty in collecting 18 percent interest on top.

The Language of Payment Terms

There are words used by credit managers, some reduced to initials, with which every businessman should be totally familiar:

Net. Terms such as "net 30" mean the face value of the invoice must be paid within 30 days of the specified date.

Open account. This implies payment within a time period previously agreed upon. It also means no advance payment or deposit is required by the seller prior to shipment of the goods or delivery of the service.

FOB. "Free on board" means that the price quoted includes delivery to or at a certain point. "FOB Destination" indicates the selling price includes delivery to the site specified by the buyer. "FOB factory" means the buyer pays delivery costs from the manufacturer's site.

COD. "Cash on delivery" is a condition under which the buyer must pay for the goods or services at the moment they are delivered. Under such terms, the seller assumes freight charges or includes them in the selling price. If the buyer refuses to pay or to accept the merchandise, the seller assumes freight charges both ways.

CIA. "Cash in advance" is required at times by the seller when for whatever reason he is unable to extend open account or COD terms to the buyer. Shipment is not made until the seller receives cash or some form of secured tender for whatever amount has been agreed upon.

SDBL. "Sight draft, bill of lading" requires the buyer to make immediate cash payment on a sight draft attached to an advance bill of lading, which is evidence of transfer of title of the merchandise from the shipper to the addressee.

EOM or MOM. "End of the month" or "middle of the month" is a condition of payment that indicates that the credit period starts either on the last day or on the fifteenth day of the month in which the goods are shipped. Using EOM terms, for example, purchases made on June 1, 8, 16, and 24 are invoiced as of July 1. Prompt payment discounts may be part of the terms. Thus, for goods shipped on June 8, the invoice may be dated July 1 and the terms may be 2/10, net 30. The full amount would not be due until July 30. Using MOM terms, the purchases made on June 1 and June 8 would be invoiced on June 15. The June 16 and June 24 purchases would be invoiced as of July 1.

Proximo. This Latin word means "next." Terms of "2/10 prox." mean if payment is made before the tenth of the month following, the purchaser may take 2 percent discount. This is the equivalent of "2/10 EOM."

ROG or AOG. "Receipt of goods" or "arrival of goods" dates the invoice at the time the buyer receives the goods.

Extra terms. Under these terms an extra period is offered for cash discounts. A typical statement is "2/10, 1/20." This means "2 percent discount if paid in ten days, 1 percent if paid in 20 days."

Terms and conditions are sometimes referred to as "boiler plate," words printed at the bottom or on the backside of a purchase contract or the invoice. Take nothing for granted. Take time to read the boiler plate, especially when doing business with a supplier for the first time.

23

How to Expand Sales Through Account Analysis

OF course, you are reading this section because you are interested in growth—expansion. You certainly don't want to get smaller; nor do you want to stand still. You may not have the slightest interest in becoming a giant corporation. But, certainly, you do want positive growth—expanded sales volume from which your firm may derive increased profits.

The best place to start planning such an expansion of sales volume is to determine the sources of expansion. Customers and prospects must be defined, qualified, quantified. Which customers are likely to increase their purchases? Which prospects are likely to become customers? Which lost accounts can be recaptured? Which inactive accounts are likely to become active?

The answers to these questions are vital, too: Which accounts have been growing, and why? Can the knowledge and experience gained from these growth accounts be applied to other accounts?

And, always keeping an eye on sales costs, can you grow without adding significantly to fixed expenses such as salaries, facilities, rent? In order to find and understand the strengths and weaknesses of your current sales efforts, you need a simple profile of your customers. You may be doing this already in an informal way; however, it is well worth the time to draw a specific evaluation of your accounts. Professional sales managers for manufacturers do this with their distributor billings on a continuing basis. The wholesaler or retailer must do this with his end-user accounts. A recommended method is *account analysis*.

Choose a period of time such as the past three to five years of selling activity. List all the accounts you have sold, by name. Try to group the accounts by market, for example, radio and TV stations, colleges, hospitals, recording studios, advertising agencies, utilities, government agencies, and so on. As in Figure 14, tabulate the sales volume for three or more of the most recent years of operation. List the current year or the equivalent 12-month period just completed.

Now, one of the keys to analysis is contained in the last two columns of the chart. These two columns are dollar comparisons between the current year and (1) the poorest of

Figure 14. Example of sales volume tabulation (in thousands of dollars).

Customer Name	1972	1973	1974	1975	1975 Compared With	
					Poorest	Best
A	$135	$138	$145	$102	$−33	$−43
B	6	9	8	10	+4	+1
C	20	21	16	17	+1	−4
D	103	123	135	155	+52	+20
E	10	8	—	—	−8	−10
Totals	274	299	304	284		
Change	—	+9%	+1.7%	−6.6%		

the previous years being reviewed, and (2) the best of the previous years being reviewed. It quantifies the direction, that is, the growth or decline, of the specific account relative to history.

This chart provides some cold, hard facts that say something like, "It's real nice to do business with good old Joe, but can I really afford it?" One of the things the chart shows is that this business has been through a peak in 1974 when it increased about 11 percent above 1972 as a reference point. Note that 1973 was 9 percent better than 1972. Why? Most of it came from account D, and through the years that account has been literally becoming the "egg in one basket." Look at the other accounts. E stopped buying from this company by 1974. A signals trouble ahead. B needs some careful re-evaluation: Will it ever grow to a significant dollar volume? Is this an area of individual opportunity? C is possibly in the same position as B. And, why is A suddenly dropping, down almost 30 percent in 1975?

Of course, this ignores the question of profitability. Maybe the profits, as a percent of sales, have grown at a rate exceeding the rate of sales increase. On the other hand, actual *dollar* profits may be disappointing, inadequate to assure a continuing ability to maintain high credit ratings; or cash flow may be too low to permit maintenance of proper inventory levels or to invest in other areas affording good returns. Individual cases have to be studied in depth, possibly in conjunction with a professional accountant.

However, getting back to the chart, listing accounts in a way similar to that just described provides a tool for drawing a picture of your present business. If accounts have become stagnant or dormant, you will want to find out why. Search for the negatives that made things go wrong. And, don't be kind to yourself. Ask some hard, searching questions. Once you know why the sales fell off, you have the clues to regain lost accounts, or to re-invigorate slow ones.

Has an inactive account just stopped buying your kind of services or hardware, or has he shifted his major buys to a competitor? If the latter is the case, why is it so? What is your competitor's appeal? What can you learn from him? Does he have superior product knowledge? Better service? Better people? Is he beating you out on price? *Wait a minute there!* If he's cutting price, try to estimate his costs and profits. It has happened before that the price cutter loses money on each sale and tries to make it up in volume.

But the customer may lose something, too. The nonprofit competitor is probably sacrificing some important ingredient like service and follow-through. Find his weakness. It is probably your strength. Sell your strength to your lost account. Betting money says your competitor may go broke and that you will recapture the account without giving away the backbone of your existence: profits on sales.

Certainly it is apparent that in this chapter we have been discussing the need to examine individual accounts in order to implement a program for expansion. Or let's call it, more formally, "defining risks and optimizing opportunities for expansion."

One can be deceived or fail to recognize opportunities if he looks only at the bottom line, the grand total of sales. Much can be learned from the accounts which have been steadily growing. Can the factors which caused their increases be used to increase sales to other accounts? If changes can be identified by industry, is this a reflection of your own selling emphasis, your product line? Or, is it a broadly recognized factor of national economics?

If you find your present strengths are identified with specific markets or industries, research your territory to locate customers who are in the same fields, but on whom you may not have been calling regularly. A source of such information is the *County Business Patterns* report of the U.S. Bureau of the Census for states in which you are active. This report shows, by industry, the number of plants in each county within a state. The plants are classified by size and number of employees. Think of these points: What percentage of the plants are you calling on? Are you actively selling? If not, why not? Check your public library for other publications offering data on industries.

Now your reaction can be (1) I don't have enough sales-men to do all this, or (2) I can't afford to add more salesmen to do this. But additional salesmen may not be needed. Consider the following thoughts and their applicability to your situation:

□ Prospecting for new business is a tough assignment, and many salesmen do not do as much of it as they could or should. Consider a special contest tied into awards for bringing in new accounts or for reactivating an inactive account.

□ Sometimes we are not aware of the added sales potential of present accounts. Suggest that each of your men ask every one of his accounts, "What can I do to become a more important supplier to you, to earn a larger share of your business?" Do it yourself, too.

□ Some salesmen are uncomfortable or not at their best with certain types of accounts, especially big-company accounts. Review your sales-account assignments periodically to assure yourself that the marriages are correct.

□ On the basis of profiles drawn of each account's dollar value, steer salesmen's energies into those areas where their time will be most productive in writing orders.

□ Make certain your salesmen, inside and outside, have top-notch knowledge of your services and products or, at least, know exactly where to get authoritative information real fast. Your salesmen must learn to talk about products and services in terms of *benefits* to their customers. The ability to recite specifications is useful, but when the recitation is stated in the form of benefits the sale comes closer to fruition.

□ Beware of overservicing bread-and-butter accounts, just as you should beware of overservicing marginal accounts.

Finally, review the chart with your salesmen. Or, if you are your own salesman, figure out how much time you actually spend with each of the accounts. Estimate the dollar productivity on an hourly basis for each account. This analysis could very easily indicate that the emphasis should be adjusted between personal and telephone contacts for specific accounts; contact marginal accounts more often by telephone. Then, you and your salesmen can spend more time increasing the business being done with highly productive accounts *and* in contacting new accounts.

Yes, it is possible to expand sales without significantly increasing selling expenses. In essence, when you examine your business in the ways suggested above, you are drawing an analysis for profits.

24

How to Create
a Positive Image

A cliché among advertising and public relations people states, "When all else fails, try honesty." Another version of the idea is "Tell it like it is." However, first one has to decide what "it" is. "It" is the image conjured in the minds of your customers and prospects at the mention or thought of your company's name, products, or services. The clever businessman can generate virtually any image he wants in the minds of his customers. He can create any sort of initial impression of what the prospective customer thinks is waiting for him if he visits the premises or purchases the products or services.

Advertising, direct mail, and public relations are tools which have created professions and industries. When used properly, they are valuable business-image builders. However, they can cause irreparable damage, literally destroy those who abuse them, misuse them, or think one can "fool all the people all the time."

It would be an oversimplification to assume that as long as they are honest, advertising and public relations can't fail. Yet, there are so many variables, only some of which are controllable in the business world, that it is naive to assume that the strongbox of success can be readily opened with just one simple key.

At some time in its life, every business, small or big, makes some use of advertising and public relations techniques. Even the smallest corner cigar store uses one of them, when the owner puts a sign in the window announcing a special such as "New! Panatelas 3 for 29¢!" He is saying that he has the *latest* at a *low price*. However, should a passerby enter the store, ask the person behind the counter for three panatelas, and be told, "Oh, they haven't come in yet," he is likely to feel deceived and next time will probably pass the store by.

What Image Do You Want?

It is practicable to build an image, create an action through advertising and public relations techniques. The first step is *not* to put together some sort of ad, place it in a local newspaper, for example, and sit back and wait for the action to take place. Businessmen who have tried this simple approach are among those who claim, "Advertising just doesn't work." The fact is, they didn't really try to make it work. These same people would correctly say it would be ridiculous to stop a stranger on the street, take him firmly by the arm, and say, "You are now one of my top salesmen!" Advertising and public relations are known as "salesmen in print." And the successful businessman is, among other things, the compleat manager of his advertising and public relations programs, his "salesmen in print." How to begin?

Every business must have its objectives, with plans, programs, and budgets designed for attainment. In the implementation of the programs, it is vital to be able to describe exactly what image or thought association is to be generated.

Using local newspapers, supermarkets and retail stores create the images in the minds of customers: "pay less," "get more," "you must be satisfied," "none better," "high fashion," "exclusive designs," "for ladies only." Through the medium of local television commercials, the automotive dealer relates his business name to "lowest prices," "fine-quality used cars," or "the largest selection." Through trade publications, a manufacturer of industrial hardware generates the impression of "quality," "uniqueness," "high technology," or "superior performance" in the minds of the readers. Almost all of them use direct mail flyers, brochures, and catalogs to reach specific neighborhoods, cities, counties, or specifiers and buyers of specialized and technical hardware.

Define and describe the spirit of the business. Boil the description and definition down to a few concise sentences or words. These now become the platform, the major theme on which the specific programs are founded.

How Does Advertising Differ from Public Relations?

Advertising is the use of media whose time, space, and materials have been paid for by the sponsor; a newspaper or magazine page, a radio or TV spot, a sign, a handbill, flyer, brochure, or mailer are examples of paid media. *Public relations,* often referred to as "PR" or "publicity," is the use of media not paid for on a measured basis such as dollars per line or per inch, or per minute. That is not to say that public relations doesn't cost you anything. Public relations, like advertising, takes careful thought and planned execution. As with advertising, there are fixed costs which must be budgeted, such as personnel wages and benefits, and variable costs, such as out-of-pocket expenses for supplies, travel, purchased services, and business entertainment.

While the sponsor of a paid advertisement may choose his timing and message—within limitations of the specific medium's availability and policies—the sponsor of a public

relations (or publicity) program is under the control of the
media toward which the effort is directed. The message
contained in the paid advertisement may be interesting in
the eyes of its sponsor, hopefully in the eyes of the reader as
well. However, the message or idea conveyed through the
public relations effort must be newsworthy in the eyes of the
people who control the media, who are more critical and
more objective than the sponsor.

There are a number of guidelines that are common to
both advertising and public relations. In small business,
both functions are usually under the control of one person,
possibly the owner or manager. In big business, it is more
usual to separate the advertising department from the public
relations department. The former spends much of its time
with the sales representatives of the various media, acquiring demographic and other statistical data which support the
purchase of time and space. The latter spends its time exclusively with editors and publishers, reporters and news com-
mentators in an effort to develop relationships that enable
the company's representative to gain the undivided attention of the media when it is believed that a newsworthy
event is in the making or has just occurred.

Except for human and mechanical errors, there are
guarantees to the sponsor of a paid advertisement that his
message will appear or be broadcast in a selected format,
with preplanned visuals, at a predetermined time and place,
for a specified length of time or space.

There are no such guarantees that a newsworthy story
will appear at all. Much depends on time and space available
within the editorial arena and on what other stories are
available; competing stories that are considered more valuable by the media will, of course, "beat out" the one that has
just been offered.

There are independent agencies and free-lance people
who specialize in advertising and public relations. They
offer a variety of services which can supplement the company's own internal departments, or which can perform virtually as *the* department. Naturally, costs are related to the

amount of time and the nature of the services purchased. Schedules of fees vary, including hourly rates for demand services, fixed fees for job agreements and annual contracts, and straight commission based on a percentage of the advertising/PR budgets.

What Can Advertising and PR Do for You?

Advertising and public relations have the same objectives: to build business, promote sales. Because of this promotional commonality, we are able to discuss their values and the methods of using them for maximum effectiveness in image building as though they were a single tool. They can:

1. Reduce selling costs while expanding the sales effort.
2. Tell an audience about the business, its people, products, and services.
3. Establish the business as a prime source for products and services.
4. Provide a method for building confidence, goodwill, and reputation.
5. Build store traffic.
6. Stimulate prospective buyers to take definitive actions, such as write for more details or for a catalog, buy by mail, telephone an order, or come to the store to make a specific purchase.
7. Build favorable reactions among stockholders, investors, bankers, and others in the financial community as a prelude to going public, offering a second stock issue, or floating a bond.

When Should They Be Used?

1. Advertising should be scheduled, planned, and budgeted for continuity and to keep the business name constantly in front of the buyers' eyes and ears.
2. Special advertisements and public relations programs

can tie in with holidays or seasonal events—
Christmas, back-to-school, summer vacation time, and
so on.
3. Special local campaigns can be developed to coincide
with a manufacturer's national program.
4. Industrial magazines' trade-show issues are appropriate times for implementing paid-media and public
relations efforts.

How Much Should You Spend?

Several leading trade magazines and some trade associations may publish data showing how much money is spent
by major advertisers in selected media. Public relations expenditures are not usually released, possibly because the
functions of public relations may vary quite widely from
company to company, even among those in the same industry. However, there are some budgetary guidelines that can
be enumerated:
1. Promotional programs are intended to increase sales.
Therefore, it is reasonable to relate the promotion
budget to the sales forecast, as a percentage of the
forecast.
2. The budget should be flexible enough to permit increases when sales actuals are falling short of forecasts, and decreases when actuals are exceeding forecasts.
3. Businesses with prior experience in promotions can
readily make use of historical data for seasonal, cyclical, and annual budgets.
4. Start-up businesses can either make use of any available industry averages for budgets as a percent of
sales, or adopt the task-force approach, which creates
an annual program and budget and then fine-tunes
both program and budget to bring them into line with
cash flow forecasts.

Where Should You Spend It?

The basic truths of this question are (1) what media are available to your specific business? (2) which media do your customers read, listen to, or watch? and (3) what do your competitors do? Here are some types of media and techniques to be considered, for both paid advertising and nonpaid public relations:

1. Newspapers: display and classified sections.
2. Magazines: general consumer, trade, association, local church, and society publications.
3. Telephone directories: Yellow Pages.
4. Direct mail: letters, cards, leaflets, catalogs.
5. Radio and television: live or prerecorded messages.
6. Outdoor: billboards, posters, signs, car cards, hand-bills.
7. Specialty items: calendars, pens, pencils, key chains, and other premiums or "remembrance" items.
8. Exhibits and shows: regional and national trade shows, local civic exhibits, airport terminal displays, traveling road shows.
9. Participation by articulate employees or executives as speakers at business or technical conferences or as panel members at seminars.

Follow Through on the Promotion Program

Extra mileage can be gained from the advertising and public relations efforts by merchandising the hard copy. Do such things as:

1. Mailing a preprint of your local newspaper ad to your charge-account customers.
2. Mailing a preprint of your general consumer or trade ad or catalog or direct mail piece to your salesmen, distributors, and retailers, thereby making them feel they are part of the team.

3. Displaying copies of the material on your bulletin board or, in a retail operation, on counters and in windows where they will gain extra readership and add to the objective of building a desirable image.
4. Doing the same with newspaper or magazine articles that report favorably and interestingly on your business or your industry.

Keep a Portfolio

You want to keep a scrapbook of advertising and PR programs, not because you are vain but because you are a professional businessman who understands the value of data analysis, records of expenditures, and the results they have brought. Copies of your advertisements, PR releases, and editorial appearances should be mounted in the book, in chronological order. The following information should be annotated:

1. Where and when the item appeared.
2. The cost in detail for creative and production charges and the direct costs of the media, where applicable.
3. Dollar information on sales increases directly attributable to the promotion program, where they can be identified.
4. A mathematical ratio of direct costs divided by identified incremental sales, where such sales have been identified with the promotion. Use this to compare the relative successes of individual programs and as a guide for future efforts.

Just the Beginning

Advertising and PR programs alone do not insure a positive image for a brand name, a product, a service, a store, or a manufacturer. Such "mechanical salesmen" can only predispose the buyer or potential customer toward a favorable reaction to what has been offered. The product or service must be truthfully described. If not, the disappointment of the buyer or prospect can produce an effect which is the exact opposite of what was desired by the sponsor. Everything the business and its employees do in contact with the "outside world" will contribute to the image. Therefore, when the image has been defined and can be clearly expressed, make certain that every employee, sales clerk, field sales and service person, checker, wrapper, porter, anyone who might meet your most important people—your customers—has been instructed in the nature of the positive image you are trying to create and in the key role of each employee in contributing to success.

25

Growth Opportunities Through Export Sales

THE demand for a great many products is rising overseas at a faster rate than in the United States. This has been true for many years, and there are no indications that the rate will slow down. All over the world new consumers of goods are appearing with rising standards of living and more money to spend. Many companies have found opportunities to increase their sales volume significantly through foreign trade.

It is possible, too, that foreign trade can be more profitable than domestic business. Many of the restrictions with which exporters have had to cope—restraints in imports placed by foreign governments as well as controls on exports by the United States government—have been removed or eased. As the demand continues to grow for American goods, there is every reason to believe the small company can make an important contribution to the elevation of living standards abroad while expanding its own profit base.

Where to Start

To say the world is a big marketplace is an understatement. It is also a complex place for the small businessman
who tries to venture far and wide geographically. However,
the experienced international marketing manager contends
that, setting language differences aside, the similarities in
structure of the selling organization overwhelm the differences. As in the United States, many overseas countries have
sales agents, manufacturers' reps, distributors, dealers, and,
of course, government agencies which buy direct from the
manufacturer. Fundamentally, selling to export markets is
not dissimiliar to selling to domestic markets. The problems
of differences in languages are becoming minimal; English
appears to be growing very rapidly as the language of international commerce.

The first place to start is with a determination of whether
or not surplus plant capacity and the need for new markets
exist today or, in the event of planned increases in facilities,
will in the predictable future become critical factors. Obviously, the plant that is operating at 100 percent capacity
today, and that forecasts no change, is in no position to search
for new markets. The second place is within the company's
own planning sessions. It is important to redefine the nature
of the product intended for overseas sales. Is it a consumer
item? An industrial item? What are the classes or categories
of customers who would purchase it? Who is the competition? What prices are charged? How is the product distrib-
uted?

Sounds very familiar, doesn't it? Of course it is. The kinds
of facts involved in foreign market research are very much
the same kinds of facts one looks for in examining domestic
markets. The major difference is in orientation of the marketer. When one looks at a map of the continental United
States, one sees outlines of the 48 states. However, the
domestic marketer is automatically inclined to think of them
as one mass market, one state being very much like the other
with some minor regional variations due to climates or population counts.

A close look at the map of the African continent, as one example, also reveals a number of boundaries. But these are outlines of total entities, nations, not states of one nation. There may be vast cultural, ethnic, religious, and economic variations from border to border. So, the international marketer in doing his research must take the continent, not as a whole but nation by nation, examining each one separately for unique opportunities. Special guidance may be needed in selecting specific markets in which the company is to concentrate its export marketing efforts.

Where Can Special Help Be Found?

The assumption is that an experienced international marketer is not regularly employed by the firm and that guidance is needed from outside sources. Following the theme of a famous advertising campaign, one could walk through the Yellow Pages of the telephone directories. This might be of some help in obtaining names of dealers, for example, in television sets or other consumer goods. Many foreign telephone directories do list major headings in the same way domestic directories display them. And some main offices of telephone companies have shelves filled with the directories of overseas cities which, interestingly, contain Yellow Pages sections that are very much like the domestic directories.

A directory search is laborious and time consuming. It will, however, provide some names and addresses for correspondence and a mail survey of wholesalers and retailers. The telephone numbers will be of little value. The costs of trying to locate sales agents by overseas telephone are prohibitive for even the largest of companies.

The U.S. Department of Commerce provides a considerable amount of economic and market data for specific countries overseas. These can be obtained directly from the Department's district offices or through government-owned and -operated bookstores situated in major cities. The Department produces many valuable publications that can

keep the businessman well informed on international commercial developments, useful to the development of export
marketing plans.

Commerce Today is a biweekly magazine which pub-
lishes information and reports on various international markets. It also contains news of specific sales opportunities.

*Foreign Economic Trends and Their Implications for the
United States* are individual country reports, prepared
semiannually by U.S. Commercial Officers stationed at
Foreign Service posts. These publications give current business conditions, current and near-term prospects, and the
latest data on growth and buying patterns.

Export Market Digests summarize the research findings
of the Department of Commerce on sales potential of specific
products in individual markets, emphasizing sales opportunities.

Global Market Surveys are a compilation of market
summaries by nation which indicate sales potentials of
specific products in growth markets. Some of the *Surveys*
have dealt with agricultural machinery; food processing
and packaging; industrial and scientific instruments; air
conditioning and refrigeration; pumps, valves, and compres-
sors; electronic data processing equipment; and biomedical
hardware.

Market Share Reports provide a five-year spread of statistical data on imports of over 1,100 commodities for 90 countries. The *Reports* also show the U.S. share of market for
approximately 1,100 commodities in major overseas markets.

There are many special publications dealing with
specific aspects of export. These include U.S. *Trade Promotion Facilities Abroad, A Guide to Financing Exports,
Overseas Trade Centers and Fairs,* and *A Basic Guide to
Exporting.*

Consultants in export, as with so many areas of business,
may be located through a chamber of commerce, a trade
association, or through others already involved actively in
export sales. Many of these people learned their trade and

developed their skills as international marketing managers for large companies. They chose the entrepreneurial route, setting up their own businesses based on special knowledge of countries, markets, or products and industries. As with other service organizations, the consultant's compensation is variable—a retainer, a project basis, fixed fee plus expenses, or a time or per diem rate when overseas travel can be combined with an assignment for a similar but nonconflicting account.

How to Use the Resources of the U.S. Department of Commerce

The Bureau of International Commerce (BIC) of the U.S. Department of Commerce has developed several valuable aids designed to help U.S. companies find overseas buyers. The aids are part of the Trade Opportunities Program (TOP) which is dedicated to locating opportunities for direct sales to buyers—private and government. The aids also contain notices of foreign companies offering to represent U.S. firms abroad. Leads which are uncovered by more than 200 overseas American embassies and consulates are telexed to the TOP computer in Washington, D.C. The Department of Commerce provides several methods of identifying foreign importers, agents, distributors, customers, or licensees:

Export Mailing List Service consists of lists retrieved for individual subscribers from the Department's computer file of foreign contacts known as the *Foreign Traders Index*. The retrieval is coded according to the subscriber's Standard Industrial Classification (SIC). The form can be a printout or gummed mailing labels.

Agent Distributor Service is offered to U.S. companies that are searching for satisfactory trade connections abroad. This service provides up to three names per country of overseas firms that have expressed a willingness to handle the subscriber's products.

Directories are available which identify *State Trading*

Organizations in countries where trade is conducted through state-owned or -controlled organizations, and *Business Firms* in selected developing countries.

World Traders Data Reports provide detailed information on overseas firms whose names might have been previously obtained, for example, from the *Printed Trade List*. These *Reports* describe the size of the firms, products handled, sales territory, and names of owners and officers. They also describe the type of organization, method of operation, general reputation in trade and financial circles, and names of any U.S. firms currently represented.

New Products Information Service advertises worldwide over the Voice of America, in a monthly newsletter, and by newspaper articles those new or unique products available for export.

American International Traders Register is a voluntary registration of U.S. firms engaged in or interested in international trade. It is used by the Department of Commerce to channel marketing information and business opportunities that match the interests of the registrant. The information provided is used by the U.S. government only for trade promotion activities.

Overseas Business Reports are published for individual countries and describe in detail the economic and marketing status of the industrialized or developing country to which the report is dedicated. These also list trade associations and are useful in developing a comprehension of a specific geographic market.

International trade fairs, or product displays, have a history that goes back hundreds of years in European countries. Worldwide, more than 800 international trade fairs are held each year. Because the costs of exhibiting overseas are prohibitive for an individual firm, the Department of Commerce sponsors an official U.S. participation in major exhibitions. In areas where there are no suitable trade fairs, the Department sponsors special solo exhibitions of American products. Such exhibitions are scheduled only when research reveals sales potential for these products. Participating U.S. business firms receive a full range of promotional and display assistance for a moderate charge.

U.S. Trade Centers, overseas "merchandise marts," or commercial showrooms have been established in 17 countries. From six to nine major product exhibitions are held annually at each center, featuring displays of up to 30 exhibitors. It is reported that it is not unusual to develop an aggregate order write-up of up to $1 million during a show, with follow-up sales as high as $20 million in the ensuing 12 months.

Catalog shows feature displays of American product catalogs, sales brochures, and graphic sales aids. These are held at U.S. embassies abroad or in conjunction with a trade fair and are an excellent way to test a foreign market for interest in a product or product line and to locate agents or distributors.

Trade missions are organized through the Department of Commerce, which develops a theme and an itinerary in countries in which there appear to be strong opportunities for sales. Through the Economic Commercial Officers of the U.S. Foreign Service posts, appointments are made with potential customers, agents, or distributors. Where necessary, interpreters are provided.

What About Special Licenses to Export?

The Export Administration Act of 1969 (with amendments) is administered by the Department of Commerce. The Act requires the President to control exports to the extent necessary to protect the national security, promote foreign policy, and conserve stocks of short-supply commodities. To improve the balance of trade and to assist the developing nations, restrictions on exports have been significantly reduced. A license document is required for a very small proportion of U.S. exports.

Unless a company's products are related to strategic commodities or, for foreign policy reasons, trade restrictions have been placed on the country of destination, it is unlikely that an export license will be required. Some commodities do come into short-supply conditions and, during those periods of short supply, temporary restrictions may be placed on export. Specific requirements can be obtained from field offices of the Department of Commerce.

How to Use Business Counseling Services of the Department

The Washington, D.C., office of the Bureau of International Commerce can provide supplemental information and personal counseling, almost to the point of laying out a small company's international marketing plan. However, for those not located near Washington, the counseling services are available through any one of the Department's 43 District Offices. It can be extremely valuable to contact them if you are (1) entering the field of export sales for the first time, (2) expanding your overseas sales, (3) trying to locate overseas sales agents or representatives, or (4) licensing your product for manufacture in a foreign country.

The Department has, in the Washington office, experts on specific commodities and countries. They can discuss specific information about economic trends, markets for particular products, basic data, and other facts which can help determine the best approaches to overseas selling.

Many of the District Offices have experienced staff personnel who will visit your plant to review with your people the many valuable services offered by the Bureau of International Commerce. They can show you samples of the publications and describe the ways in which they may be put to work for you. Also, they can help you determine your SIC code number, an important aid to locating relevant data through government agencies.

All this, at no charge, is a resource that any small-business manager should investigate from the very moment he begins to consider how his company might successfully share in the expanding opportunities of overseas sales.

26

How to Be Your Own Management Consultant

WHATEVER image may be conjured in one's mind by the word "consultant," the fact remains that it is descriptive of one who gives *professional* and *specialized* advice and service. As with all things, trades and skills included, there are the good and there are the inept. The best consultants, those with outstanding references of practical as well as theoretical backgrounds, command significant fees. The lower-grade consultants may command lower fees, but following their advice can bring inadequate results. It is reasonable to state that in the long run the inadequate consultant might be more expensive than the best.

However, there are times and conditions which make it impracticable to lay out cash for fees and expenses for *any* outside consultant services. It is possible to do some or all of one's own consulting work by using resources that may be as close as just down the street—the libraries.

Libraries come in many varieties. There are public libraries operated by cities, counties, states, and the federal government. The federal government is a prolific publisher of material through the Government Printing Office. Depositories of GPO publications are located throughout the country, in sections of public and university-owned libraries. Virtually every public and private school, through the college and university levels, maintains a reference or a circulation section which may be accessed by the public. Other libraries are maintained by public, commercial, and privately endowed research institutes. There are libraries maintained by corporations for internal use. Trade and professional associations and labor organizations often operate libraries which contain material related to their specific fields of endeavor. There are commercial libraries supported by industrial sponsors or by those who are willing to pay reasonable fees for the use of the resources. Religious organizations and historical societies, too, are among those that have established libraries, many of which are open to the public at no charge or for small donations.

A library is a storehouse of information, containing answers or guidance for the owners and managers of small businesses. Through their books, periodicals, and pamphlets they can help solve many of the everyday problems which beset the owner-managers.

The library is filled with expert knowledge. For example, the library has the names, addresses, and descriptions of numerous prospective buyers and sales agents all over the world. Libraries offer details and illustrations of the latest patents, copyrights, and trademarks. They can fill the innovative mind with suggestions for new products and services. Marketing expertise and statistical information of fantastic variety are there for the looking. If entering a library with its myriad of book-filled racks and free-standing card indexes seems a bit overwhelming, there are "guides," librarians who are always on the spot and eager to point the way to the material best suited to the need. Amazingly, most of it is free, or the charges, if any, would not strain the thinnest budgets.

Visit the Library

Perhaps it has been a long time since the owner or manager of the small business has been near a library. Surprisingly, many businessmen do not even know where the nearest public library is located. Obviously, a telephone directory is the first place to go to find a library whose name and location are usually listed after the name of your city in the white pages. Or you might look in the Yellow Pages under the heading "Libraries" or "Library Research." A brief visit and talk with the reference librarian should convince anyone about the vast resources of information available just for the asking.

Obviously, there is no one library that can hold all the books that have been published. If the library does not have a specific, potentially valuable newspaper, magazine, pamphlet, or book on the premises, it may be possible to obtain a copy through what is known in some areas as the "interagency library loan" service; one library borrows from another, arranging for both delivery and return of the material at no charge to the borrower.

Information by Telephone

Some libraries offer assistance by telephone. If the question asked by the caller does not require extensive research time, the reference librarian may look for the answer and give it over the telephone or give the caller a list of publications located in the library which are most likely to contain the best answers. A call can often save time-consuming trips to the library to get a single fact, such as the name of a firm, its address, a listing of the key executives, number of employees, sales volume—all of which (and more) may be found in a single business directory. For some types of information, or where more than a few details are needed, it may be more prudent to visit the library rather than depend on the telephone.

Librarians—Professional Researchers

A staff member of a public library often can suggest sources and publications that are new to the most experienced user of library resources. Many people, men and women, have made a study and a career of the library. They are not there only to earn their livelihoods; they gain job satisfaction each time they succeed in locating material containing answers to questions and solutions to problems.

The small businessman can tap sources of information through business library services or the business book section of his local library. The "consulting services" of some of the world's leading experts are readily available to anyone who recognizes and uses these enormous resources.

Reading, by itself, is not an insurance policy for successful business management. Neither is the employment of a management consultant a guarantee of positive results. However, the acquisition of statistical data, the collecting of facts, the reading of theory—as a basis for practice—can significantly increase the probability that the small-business manager will attain his objectives, generally described as "success."

Afterword

WORDS, sentences, paragraphs, chapters, and books have described in depressing detail the reasons why small businesses fail. Perhaps the positive view is just the negative turned inside out. Whatever, it is appropriate to close this book with a description of some of the traits that characterize the owner or manager of a small business that succeeds:

Motivation. The entry and survival of a new business must be based on a logical development of the individual's desire to own or manage his business. Spur-of-the-moment actions, or reacting to the "just thought I'd try it" syndrome, or hopping from paid employment to self-employment are counterproductive.

Expectations. Of course, one must have high expectations, but the realist—the one who has done research so that he has a sound basis for forecasting sales volume, expenses, and growth opportunities—is moving in a positive direction.

Flexibility. More than "rolling with the punches," this means foreseeing and anticipating change, and having the managerial know-how to take corrective actions.

Managerial know-how. Academic training in business management can be an excellent foundation for the effective manager of tomorrow's business. However, just suppose one was allowed to choose only between a business school and an active occupation as the training ground for going into one's own business. A successful employment record with progressive promotions may be more conducive to commercial success than a progressive accumulation of A grades and diplomas. Ideally, if time and finance permit, academic combined with occupational achievement can be exceptionally advantageous.

Persistence and stamina. Sticking with it, persisting, refusing to quit without trying all possible solutions, is essential to growth. And, of course, the physical demands of the growth-oriented manager's job require stamina.

Personality. It is fact that some people are better suited to a certain assignment than are others. The manager of a retail establishment, for example, who must come in contact with the general public is tuned to success if his personality and self-discipline make the contact a pleasant experience for the customer. Nobody likes to deal with a sourpuss or a malodorous or unkempt person. It is important to *think* positively in the business world—and to *look* positive.

Adequate capital resources. One occasionally reads about the person who "parlayed $1,000 into my first $1 million." Setting that infrequent phenomenon aside, it is important to have finances on hand—or available when needed. Such resources enable the owner-manager to operate on a sound basis, for example, to purchase in economic lots; take advantage of trade or cash discounts; maintain the proper level of fixed assets, equipment, machinery, and facilities; and attract the right kind of people with the appropriate level of experience to assure intelligent planning and execution of programs.

Businesses succeed because all of the above characteristics are found among the personality traits of their managers. One must have all, not just one or two of them. Point to the sole proprietor who has all of these characteristics and you point to a probable winner. Point to the active business partners who complement each other neatly to totalize these characteristics and you have a winning team. Identify the corporation whose top-management team combines these characteristics and the results will probably be reflected in a statement of positive earnings.

Point to yourself. Do you have them?

Index

accountability records, 30
account analysis, sales
    expansion through,
    223–228
accounting system, need for, 27
    see also bookkeeping process
accounts payable, 56
accounts receivable, 56, 127
    credit and, 174
accounts receivable aging test,
    31, 34, 57
accounts receivable control,
    33–34
accrued expenses, 57–58
acid-test ratio, 148
acquisition, cost of, 233–235
advertising
    cost of, 233–235
    false and deceptive, 117
    follow through on, 235–236
    as image builder, 229
    vs. public relations, 231–233
Agent Distributor Service, 243

AICPA, see American Institute
    of Certified Public
    Accountants
allowances, defined, 58
American Institute of Certified
    Public Accountants, 55
American International Traders
    Register, 244
anticompetitive mergers,
    115–116
antitrust laws, 111–112
antitrust practices, 120–122
assets
    in balance sheet, 125–129
    current, 59, 147
    depreciation of, see
        depreciation
    sale of, 87–88

bad debt, reserve for, 56
balance sheet, 125–129
    defined, 60
    see also financial statements

253

balance sheet approach, to
 business plan, 12
bank loans, 170–171, 177
bank reconciliation, 31
bids, job specifications and, 90
bookkeeping process,
 information for, 27–28
 see also accounting system
book value, defined, 83–85
borrowing, short- vs. long-term,
 171
 see also financing; money
break-even analysis, 62–63
 limitations of, 63–64
break-even chart, 65–69
 drawing of, 65–67
 dynamic input type, 68–69
 use of, 69
break-even point, defined, 62,
 67
brokerage, payment of to buyer,
 118
budget, expense, *see* expense
 budget
Bureau of International
 Commerce, 243, 246
business
 marketing conditions and
  requirements of, 13–14
 nature of, 13
business classification, 14
business failures, cause of, 1
business finance, vocabulary of,
 55–56
business form
 life of, 39–40
 risk and, 37–39
business plan
 anticipated orders and sales
  in, 21–22

"balance sheet" approach to,
 12
 benefits of, 10
 cash or credit operations in,
  19
 competitors and, 15
 cost reduction effect in, 22
 distribution system in, 16
 manufacturing operations
  and, 16–17
 market area in, 14
 money requirements in,
  19–21
 monthly expenses in, 20
 need for, 7–10
 overhead in, 17–18
 partner in, 18
 space needs for, 17–18
 Standard Industrial
  Classification in, 14
 turnover rate and, 17

capital resources, need for, 252
cash
 defined, 56
 working, vs. capital, 158
cash budget, 161–164
cash flow, 159–160
 billing cycle and, 164–165
cash flow budget, 165–166
cash forecast, 56–57
cash needs, 19–21, 157–166,
 167–171
cash-receipts journal, 30–31
cash records, 30–32
cash register, sales slip from, 29
Celler Amendment (1950),
 115–116
Census Bureau, 190, 226
certified public accountants, 55

CIA payment, defined, 221
Clayton Act (1913), 111–115,
    117
COD, defined, 221
Commerce Department, U.S.,
    190
  export sales and, 241–242
  resources of, 243–246
Commerce Today, 242
competition
  mergers and, 115–116
  pricing and, 98, 111–112
  unfair, 111
competitors
  advantages over, 15–16
  in business plan, 15
  strengths and weaknesses of,
    15
complacency, cost estimating
    and, 93–94
contribution pricing, 105
corporation
  form of, 37
  life of, 37, 39
  risk and, 38–39
cost control authority,
    delegation of, 76
cost estimating
  complacency in, 93–94
  danger signals in, 89–94
  job duration in, 93
  job specifications in, 90
  morale in, 93
  overhead in, 92
cost of sales, defined, 58
cost reduction, 71–79
  defined, 72
  delegation in, 76
  planning in, 76–77
  profit improvement and, 89

costs
  defined, 64–65
  distribution, 73–74
  equipment, 91
  fixed, 65
  marketing, 74–75
  of materials and labor, 90–91
  order-getting, 75
  of replacement, vs.
    acquisition, 88
  semivariable, 65
  sources of data in, 65
  variable, 64–65, 95
County Business Patterns, 226
CPA, *see* American Institute of
    Certified Public
    Accountants
credit
  in business plan, 19
  cash flow and, 164
  financial statement and, 133
  information needed for,
    174–177
  profitability measurement
    and, 154–155
credit agencies and reports, 191
creditors, short- and long-term,
    154–155
credit records, 31
current assets, 59, 147
current liabilities, 59, 150
current ratio, 147, 150
customer relations
  public relations and, 231–235
  salesmen and, 197–198
  service technician and, 45–48
customers, choosing of,
    114–115

daily cash reconciliation, 30

daily sales summary, 29
debt capital, 148
debt ratio, 148
depreciation, 81–88
    defined, 81–82
    deterioration and, 86
    income and, 86–87
    inflation and, 88
    judgment in, 85–86
    obsolescence and, 86
    reserve for, 59
    and sale of asset, 88
depreciation cost, 83
depreciation guidelines, 85–86
depreciation methods, 83–85
    comparison of, 84
deterioration, 82
    depreciation and, 86
direct mail, 229
disability insurance, 50
discount pricing, 106–107
discounts
    quantity, 219
    seasonal, 219
    trade, 218–219
    types of, 217–218
distribution cost analysis, 73–74
distribution network in
    business plan, 16
distributor-service
    organizations, service
    technician and, 45–48
double declining balance
    method, 83–85
dumping, 105
Dun & Bradstreet reports, 191
dynamic input break-even
    chart, 68–69

emotion-demand factor, pricing
    and, 95

employee benefits record, 33
employee-earnings and
    withholdings, 32
employee laws, 48–50
employee records, 32–33
employees
    advances to, 56
    hiring of, 41–45
    optimum number of, 41
employment agencies, 44
employment applications file,
    32
EOM payment, defined, 222
Equal Pay Act, 49
equipment costs, 91
equipment records, 33
equity capital, debt and, 148,
    171
exclusive deals, 117
expectations, realist approach
    and, 251
expense allowances, record of,
    32
expense budget, 77–79
expense dollars, analysis of,
    72–73
expenses
    accrued, 57–58
    in financial statement, 134
    operating, 58
Export Administration Act
    (1969), 245
Export Mailing List Service,
    243
export sales, 239–246
    licenses for, 245–246
    special help for, 241–242
    special publications on, 242

factors, credit from, 170
Fair Labor Standards Act, 48

fair trade agreements, 113–114
Federal Bureau of
    Investigation, 121
Federal Trade Commission,
    112–113, 116, 119
    guides of, 118
    law enforcement by, 116–117
Federal Trade Commission Act
    (1914), 111–113
FICA tax, 49
finance, 53–180
financial publications, 191
financial statements
    critical analysis of, 133–139
    limitations of, 133
    need for, 27–28
    profitability and, 143–144
    reading of, 123–125
    in return on investment,
        139–140
    uses of, 135
financial terms, 55–60
financing, sources of, 173–180
    see also bank loans;
        borrowing; money
financing institutions, private,
    178–180
fixed assets, 126–127
    credit and, 175
    defined, 59
fixed-assets/tangible net worth
    ratio, 153
fixed costs, 65
fixed expenses, in break-even
    chart, 66
fixtures and property records,
    33
flexibility, need for, 251
flexible markup pricing, 98
flexible pricing, 98

Ford, Gerald R., 114
FOB, defined, 221
forecasting, sales, see sales
    forecasting
foreign sales, see export sales
Foreign Trades Index, 243

government agencies, financing
    by, 177–180
Government Printing Office
    publications, 248
gross profit, 30
    defined, 58
    see also profit
gross profit percentage, 146
gross sales, defined, 58
growth, organizing of, 35–40

hiring procedure, 43–45
honesty, in self-evaluation, 12
hours worked record, 32

image
    advertising and public
        relations in, 230–233
    control of in business plan,
        18–19
    positive, 229–237
incentive programs, 207
income tax
    corporation and, 36–37
    deduction of, 49
    net profit and, 36
inflation, depreciation and, 88
insurance records, 33
Internal Revenue Service, 36,
    49
inventory, defined, 57
inventory control records, 28
inventory loss, 127

job description, 32, 43
  sales candidate and, 198–199
  training and, 47
job specification, in cost
  estimating, 90
journals and ledgers, in
  bookkeeping process, 27
Justice Department, U.S., 111,
  117
  Antitrust Division of,
  120–122

labor costs, 91
labor needs, in business plan,
  17
ledger, in bookkeeping process,
  27
liabilities, current, vs.
  long-term, 59–60
libraries, use of, 248–250
limitations, acceptance of, 12
liquidity
  defined, 147
  vs. solvency, 148
liquidity ratio, 147
loans
  bank, 170–71
  short-term, 171
  see also borrowing; credit;
  money
long-term investments,
  defined, 58–59
long-term liabilities, 59–60
loss, defined, 62

McGuire Amendment (1952),
  113
management, 53–180
management consulting,
  "do-it-yourself" form of,
  247–250

manufacturing operations, in
  business plan, 16–17
marketable securities, defined,
  57
market area, in business plan,
  14
marketing and sales, 181–250
marketing conditions, in
  business plan, 13–14
marketing cost analysis, 74–75
market price, 96–97
market share, estimating of,
  189–190
Market Share Reports, 242
market size, estimate of,
  188–189
material costs, 91
mergers, competition and,
  115–116
Miller-Tydings Amendment
  (1937), 113
money
  kinds of needed, 167–171
  requirements for, in business
  plan, 19–21
  see also cash; credit
monthly expenses, in business
  plan, 20
monthly orders and sales, 21–22
Moody's service, 191
morale, in profit improvement,
  93
mortgages payable, 57
motivation, need for, 251

National Industrial Conference
  Board, 191
net income percentage, 146
net profit, 30
  defined, 58
  income tax and, 36

tangible net worth and,
        151–152
net profit/net sales ratio, 154
net sales, 58
net sales/inventory ratio, 152
net worth, tangible, 150–152
new employees, hiring of,
        43–45
new product, pricing of,
        102–105
New Product Information
        Service, 244
notes payable, 56
notes receivable, 56

objective, vs. plan, 8
obsolescence, 82
Occupational Safety and Health
        Act (1970), 17
open-to-buy record, 28
operating expenses, 58
        estimate of, 162
operating plan, 30
operating profit, 58
other assets, defined, 59
other expenses, defined, 58
other income, defined, 58
out-of-stock sheet, 28
overhead
        in business plan, 18
        contribution to, 105
        in cost estimating, 92
Overseas Business Reports, 244
overtime, need for, 42

P&L statement, see
        profit-and-loss statement
        see also financial statements
partnership, 18, 37–38
payment, terms of, 219–222
pay periods, state laws and, 50

penetration pricing, 103–104
performance appraisal records,
        33
perpetual item inventory
        control, 28
persistence, need for, 252
personal balance sheet, 12
personality, positive, 252
personnel needs
        determining of, 41–42
        vs. overtime or temporary
        help, 42–43
petty cash fund, 31
PIP, see profit improvement
        programs
plan
        development of, 11–23
        vs. objective, 8
        operating, 30
planning, 5–51
        cost control and, 76–77
        need for, 8–9
        by professional salesmen,
        213–215
positive image, creation of,
        229–237
prepaid expenses, 57
price, value and, 106
price book, 29
price discrimination, 117
price fixing, 117
price increases, 107–109
price wars, 109
pricing, 95–122
        adding or dropping products
        in, 104–105
        antitrust practices and,
        120–122
        contribution, 105
        of comparable merchandise,
        118

comparative, 119
competition and, 111–112
complaints about, 109
discounting in, 106–107
discriminatory, 120–122
dumping and, 105
emotion-demand factor in, 95
exclusive deals and, 114
"factory" or "wholesale," 119
fictitious, 118–119
flexible, 98
full-cost, 97
going rate, 99
gouging and, 96
gross margin, 99
market price and, 96
of new products and services,
    102–105
penetration, 102–104
predatory practices and, 121
preticketing in, 119
price image in, 106–107
price increases and, 107–109
for profit, 95–109
profiteering and, 96
profit margins in, 101
"reduced," 118
resale, 113–114
and return on investment, 96
of services, 99–101
skimming, 102
two-for-one, 119
variable costs and, 95
profit
cost reduction and, 71–79
defined, 62
full cost pricing and, 97
gross, 58
as major objective, 61
measurement of, 64
as motivation, 11

need for, 61–62
net, see net profit
operating, 58
profitability measurement
key ratios in, 150–154
ratio analysis in, 143–155
profit-and-loss record, for
salespersons, 30
profit-and-loss statement, 60,
    129–132
profit barrier, breaking of,
    61–69
profit improvement programs,
    79
cost reduction and, 89
morale in, 93
progress, planning for, 76–77
proprietorship, 37
personnel needs of, 41
risk and, 38
public relations, 229
vs. advertising, 231–233
cost of, 233–235
purchase order file, 28–29
purchasing records, 28–29

quantity discounts, 219
quick assets, 148
quick ratio, 148

ratio analysis, 144–146
in profitability measurement,
    143–155
record keeping, 25–34
cost reduction in, 73
tax returns and, 26
recruiting and training, 41–51
see also training
reduced price, markup and, 118
replacement cost, 88
reported earnings, 133

resale price maintenance, 113
resale value, 85
reserve for depreciation, 59
returned goods file, 29
return on investment, 137–142
  asset investment in, 141
  formulas for, 139–141
returns, defined, 58
risk, business form and, 37–39
Robinson-Patman Act (1936),
  105, 114, 117, 122
ROI, see return on investment
rolling forecast, 193–195

salary, net profit and, 36
sale, conditions of, 217–222
sales
  cost of, 58
  expansion of, 223–228
  net, 58
sales contests, 207
sales forecasting, 183–196
  accuracy of, 191–195
  for failure or success, 187
  market size and, 188–189
  rolling of, 193–195
  sources of data in, 190–191
  targets in, 195–196
  by ultimatum, 186–187
sales meetings, training in, 205
salesmen
  average day of, 211
  enthusiasm of, 205–206
  financial motivation in, 206
  intelligence of, 200
  job description for, 198
  key-town operation by, 216
  motivation of, 206–208
  personal traits of, 201
  planning by, 213–215
  self-starting, 199

skip-stop operation of, 216
telephone and, 212–213
time and territory of, 211–216
training of, 197–209
sales promotion, 229–236
sales records, 29–30
  training and, 204
sales training, 201–209
  field sales supervisor in, 204
salvage value, 85
savings and loan associations,
  177
self-criticism, need for, 12
selling techniques, in training
  program, 203
semivariable costs, 65
service life, of asset, 85
service technician, training of,
  45–48
Sherman Antitrust Act (1890),
  111–113
SIC, see Standard Industrial
  Classification
skimming pricing, 102–103
small business
  failure of, 1
  motivation in, 11–12
  record keeping by, 25–34
  see also business plan
Small Business Administration,
  1
  loans from, 177–178
Social Security Act, 49
solvency, tests of, 148–149
sources of supply, in business
  plan, 17
space needs, in business plan,
  17
Standard Industrial
  Classification, 14
state employee laws, 49–50

straight-line depreciation, 83
success, factors in, 251–252
supplier file, 29
supply sources, 17

tangible net worth, 150–152
  fixed assets and, 153
taxes
  provisions for, 58
  salary and, 36
  withholding, 32, 49
technician, service, 45–48
telephone, use of, 212–213,
  249–250
temporary help, 42–43
terminations, reasons for, 33
terms of sale, 217–222
total debt, tangible net worth
  and, 153
total expense, 67
trade credits, 169–171
trade discounts, 218
trade fairs, 244
trade missions, overseas, 245
Trade Opportunities Program,
  243
trade schools, 44

training, 201–209
  of new employees, 44–45
  of salesmen, 197–209
  of technical service
    employee, 45–48
trial balance, 27
turnover rate, in business plan,
  17

unemployment insurance, 50
unfair business practices, 116
useful life, of asset, 85

variable costs, 64
  pricing and, 95
venture capital organizations,
  180
Veterans Administration loans,
  179

Wheeler-Lea Act (1938), 116
withholding records, 32, 49
working capital, turnover of,
  151
work in process, 57
workmen's compensation, 50
World Trades Data Reports, 244

years-digits depreciation, 85

AMACOM Executive Books-Paperbacks

Dudley Bennett	TA and the Manager	$4.95
Warren Bennis	The Unconscious Conspiracy	$4.95
Borst & Montana, Eds.	Managing Nonprofit Organizations	$5.95
J. Douglas Brown	The Human Nature of Organizations	$3.95
Ronald D. Brown	From Selling to Managing	$4.95
Richard E. Byrd	A Guide to Personal Risk Taking	$4.95
Logan M. Cheek	Zero-Base Budgeting Comes of Age	$6.95
Richard R. Conarroe	Bravely, Bravely in Business	$3.95
James J. Cribbin	Effective Managerial Leadership	$4.95
Saul W. Gellerman	Motivation and Productivity	$5.95
Bernard Haldane	Career Satisfaction and Success	$3.95
John W. Humble	How to Manage by Objectives	$4.95
Philip R. Lund	Compelling Selling	$4.95
Dale D. McConkey	No-Nonsense Delegation	$4.95
Robert J. McKain, Jr.	Realize Your Potential	$4.95
Donald E. Miller	The Meaningful Interpretation of Financial Statements	$5.95
Hank Seiden	Advertising Pure and Simple	$4.95
Leon A. Wortman	Successful Small Business Management	$4.95